SONGS OF A
WAR BOY

SONGS OF A WAR BOY

DENG THIAK ADUT

with BEN MCKELVEY

LOTHIAN

A Lothian Children's Book
Published in Australia and New Zealand in 2019
by Hachette Australia
(an imprint of Hachette Australia Pty Limited)
Level 17, 207 Kent Street, Sydney NSW 2000
www.hachettechildrens.com.au

10 9 8 7 6 5 4 3 2 1

 A catalogue record for this
book is available from the
National Library of Australia

ISBN: 978 0 7344 1962 0 (paperback)

Cover design by Christabella Designs
Front cover images courtesy Getty Images; © Telegraph Media Group Limited/David Blair.
Back cover image by Melissa Mai
Map design by Christabella Designs
Text design by Bookhouse, Sydney
Typeset in 11.8/17.6 pt Sabon LT Pro by Bookhouse, Sydney
Printed and bound in Australia by McPherson's Printing Group

To my mum, Athieu Akau Deng,
aka youhyouh, my galaxy.

And to my brother, John Mac, who rescued me.
Everything I do is to make your sacrifices worthwhile.

CONTENTS

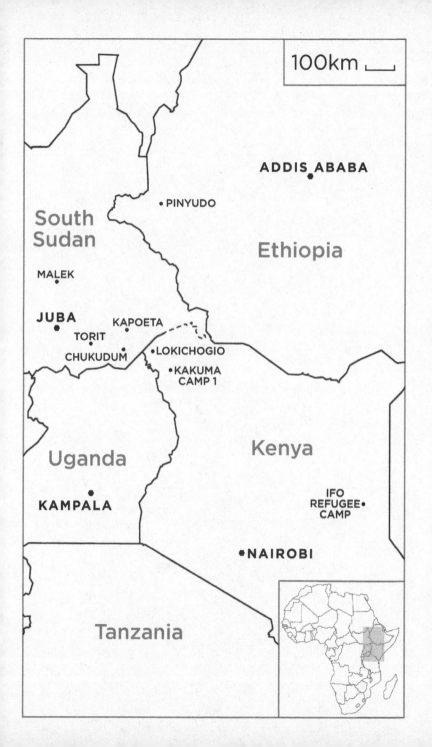

PROLOGUE

Songs are of great importance to my people, the Dinka. They precede us, introduce us and live on after we die. They are also how our deeds escape our villages, and they pass on our code of morality, culture and law.

When I was a boy I dreamed of having my own songs, but now I am a man, and I have no songs. It's likely I never will, in the traditional sense. For the Dinka, these songs are only for men. In the eyes of my culture, I am still a boy.

At a time when I should have been going through the rituals of manhood, I was caught in a vicious war. By the time I was returned to my people, I was very much a westerner. I never completed the rites of passage that are required to become a Dinka man, and so in the eyes of some of my people I am half made.

I know I am whole, though. Yes, I've had a difficult life. I'm proud of some of the things I have done, and ashamed of others, but I own all of it, and I've reconciled with all of it. That's why I am whole.

Perhaps this book could be my songs.

Perhaps my songs could also be songs for the other boys who were taken from their villages and mothers.

Ideally, every war boy should be able to sing his own songs, but so many are dead, and so many who have survived have no voice. Even though I hesitate to collectively recognise my brothers, I feel that any one of them who wants to share my verses should be able to do so because there should be songs for everybody, even the war boys.

The chapters in this book are the verses of my songs. The songs of Deng Thiak Adut, the songs of a war boy.

One

THE DINKA-BOR

I was born lucky. I was born as part of a large family, and belonged to a strong tribe. We are the Dinka-Bor – that's the name that's mostly used for us. The language we speak is also called Dinka. There is another name for us as a people, but that name is too strong to be used much. Some names, like some songs, are too powerful for their own good.

I will say it here, once, but I will say it softly. We are the *Mony Jieng*, which means the 'men of humanity'.

I was born into a village that was not built for us Dinka-Bor but for our long-horned cattle, which are sacred to my people. The cattle mean everything to us. They are our livelihood. They bless the body, the land and the soul. They would die without us, and we would not be Dinka-Bor without them.

I was born amidst the cattle in a *luak*, a grass-made cattle shed near a village called Malek. A family of swallows watched on as my mother birthed me, and others offered gentle encouragement. I took some of the soul of one of the birds as I took my first breaths, and in doing so I also took their name: *Aolouch*, or Little Swallow.

In my village, the men practise polygamy. This means they can have multiple wives at the same time. This is common among the Dinka-Bor. Men of high social standing can have as many as fifty to one hundred wives.

My mother, Athieu Akau Deng, had only recently married my father, and she was his sixth wife. As the newest wife, she was considered important. The women whom my father had previously married were also my mothers, but they were not Athieu Akau Deng. My mother had status, reputation, but also poise and wisdom.

Athieu means 'born with a struggle', Akau means 'support and fealty' and Deng means 'god of the rain'. All names speak to who my mother is.

In my village, my father, Thiak Adut Garang, was considered a prosperous man. He was a fisherman, but he also had a banana farm, and owned many cattle, all of whom he could recognise at a glance.

If a man wished to marry a woman like my mother, he needed to own a great herd of cattle. In my culture the husband pays the wife's family in cows.

My mother's clan – the Dinka-Adol – are known for having some of the most powerful women in all the Dinka lands, and my mother was tall and strong, even when standing next to her tribeswomen. I don't know what my father paid for my mother, but it would have been quite a stampede!

Athieu Akau Deng, my mother, is still a powerful woman, although now she's an old woman, so her power lies in her eyes, not her body.

My father was alive when I was born, but he died when I was still young, before I could remember him. He died of old age, which was the way many people used to die in my village.

I know about my father mostly because of the songs the other men in my village sang about him – with the finest being a tale of how he hunted a hippopotamus with his spear, and fed the entire village for days.

When he died, he was buried near our *luak*, and I would often think about him when I walked past it. In our village, men were the exclusive holders of male

5

wisdom, so my mothers couldn't tell me the stories of my father. But my brothers, some of whom had spent twenty or thirty years with him, would spend long afternoons singing his songs and telling his stories.

My brothers told me my father was a great hunter and fisherman. He was a fighter, too. Our tribe had long been in conflict with another clan called the Palek, and there was a story I especially enjoyed that involved my father throwing a Palek warrior into a smouldering pile of cow dung. I liked to hear that story over and over, waiting impatiently for the buttock-burning conclusion, which would always have me in fits of laughter.

My brothers would tell me that, after the chief (a position that rotated around the four most powerful families in the village), my father was one of the most respected men in our part of the world. The weight of his name, Thiak, was considerable, and as the eldest surviving son of my father's last wife, it is mine.

Of all my names, it is the one I am perhaps most proud of, and the fact that that name is now on the cover of this book makes me immeasurably proud.

Two

THE GOD EATER

There was another piece of great fortune that was handed to me when I was born, and that was that my mother gave birth next to the White Nile River, an endless brown–green band flowing south to north that deserves tribute from all who are alive, man or beast.

There is no life without the Nile, and no Nile without rain. The God of Rain, Deng, is one of the most powerful deities in our world. For the Dinka-Bor, life comes and goes on the ebb of Deng's mood.

My first memories are of the creatures that came to the Nile to hunt or drink. I especially loved the large Nile eagles, which would soar high over the river, as though they were the fingers of a dancing man, before carving through the air, smashing into the water and emerging with a catfish struggling between the sharp points of their claws.

To be able to simply reach into the brown of the water and bring out food like that was powerful magic as far as I was concerned. I knew men like my father could also pull food from the river, but for them it seemed like toil.

It was no more effort for the Nile eagle to fish than it was for the sun to plod across the sky each day.

One of my first fully formed memories was of a fight between two Nile eagles. One had pinched a fat, glistening fish from the river, and the other had attempted to steal his friend's quarry. Their claws locked mid-air and they spiralled down, as though both had suddenly lost the ability to fly.

The eagles landed heavily in front of Ayuen Kon, one of my mothers, who was sitting with me near the river. I felt the hurt in the animals' bodies when I heard their landing. Even as an infant, I understood that animals that lived in the sky did not need to have heavy bones, or tough skin.

My mother approached the eagles, which were chirping mournfully and quietly. Their claws were still locked, and they no longer had the strength to untangle themselves from each other. Ayuen spoke to the large birds softly, and I was stunned to find that the eagles allowed her to pull their claws apart. Eagles are not like dogs, and usually do not listen to what humans have to say.

When they were freed from each other, the eagles walked around slowly, but did not fly.

'Fly! Fly!' I said to them in hushed tones. My longing for the birds to be in the sky again was perhaps my first real wish.

My mother went to our hut, returning with a gourd of water. She poured some drops into each animal's beak. That seemed to calm them. They were still for some minutes, until one bird postured, spread its wings, let out a cry and took to the sky. The other eagle watched for a moment, and then followed, up and away. After a few moments circling above the river, both eagles disappeared from view.

I watched the spot where I'd last seen the birds and I wondered how I would feel if I suddenly found myself stuck up in the sky. I stared at the sky for some time afterwards, long past the length of my mother's patience. I stared and stared and stared and thought about flying, until I was called to eat.

It was a rare event that I had to be called to eat.

I was only *Aolouch*, little swallow, until I was given the nickname *Acham-Nhialic*. This came about because, one day as I lay on my back with some of my brothers, I mused out loud that if I could catch and kill *Nhialic*, the big god who was made out of the sky, we would have enough food for the entire village to eat. More than that, I continued, there would be leftovers forever.

For a minute my brothers were silent, not sure whether to be shocked by my talk of killing a powerful god, or to find it funny. They decided on the latter and burst out laughing. From that moment on I was called *Acham-Nhialic*, or the God Eater.

In my very young years, almost all of the trouble in my life stemmed from being constantly hungry. I would cry and whine at night if, at the end of the day, my belly wasn't as full as the river after the rains. If there was food in the pot, I would always be trying to cram fish or *ugali* (a delicious dough made of maize flour and water) into my mouth – even if I was full and the food was just tumbling out of my crammed mouth and onto the floor. I was a greedy child!

When there was a great kill – an antelope, or a crocodile, or perhaps even a hippopotamus – the meat was distributed according to family status. As a child I had no rights to any of the great kill meat, except that which my mothers or brothers would give to me. Often, however, I would eat better than some of the adults as it was easier to feed me than listen to my whining.

I often thought gristly antelope meat was a meagre consolation for one who wished to eat the biggest god of them all, but I would never refuse food, regardless of what it was.

I remember one afternoon deciding to chew on some scattered cornhusks that had been tossed on the ground, which were also being enjoyed by a troop of wild baboons. When the monkeys and I had finished our meal, I decided we were compatriots, so I led them through our gate and into our *luak* so we could all search for another course together.

When one of my mothers came into the *luak* and discovered a barrel of monkeys and a greedy little child sharing the precious fresh corn supplies, well, both species quickly learnt what the wrath of a mother could be! The baboons fled, and I got a hiding.

Even though it was I who had led the baboons into the *luak*, after that I was suspicious of the baboons. They had tricked me, I felt, and when I saw them I looked at them with narrowed eyes, no longer trusting their friendship.

One day some of my brothers and I made a bow and some arrows to shoot at the larger bugs and beetles near the river. After seeing how true the arrows flew, I decided I would get even with those monkeys that had caused my buttocks to be whipped.

I waited for two of the baboons to start mating, then I let loose with an arrow, right at the point where their bodies met. I hit the male baboon. He reared up in outrage, and then instantly identified where the attack had come from. He sized me up and decided I was an opponent of manageable size.

The baboon ran at me, screeching a song of violence. He was fast, but, moving with both hands and feet, he couldn't really attack me until he sat down. When he did, I would dart away from him. It was a high-stakes game of tag that I started to understand could have very painful repercussions.

I was saved once again by a mother, and once again my bottom felt an angry mother's wrath.

The time that my stomach led me into the gravest danger was down at the Nile, where I used to play with a couple of village girls named Akuol and Nyandit. The three of us used to wade into the water, at the mouth of an irrigation tunnel, and there I would try to catch, with my hands, any fish unlucky enough to travel through the tunnel.

When I would manage to grab a fish, I would bite into its belly, spitting out the skin, scales and bones and swallowing the delicious pink–white flesh. I thought the only danger in that game was that escaped fish would bite my testicles, but there was another, greater danger. I didn't know that some fish were not nourishing. I didn't know that some fish had flesh that would attack my stomach with a thousand knives.

I was sick for weeks after eating one particularly evil fish. I could not eat, could not move, and there were concerns that I would be joining my father under a mound next to the *luak*. I survived, but those weeks were the closest I'd been to dying until the war came to our village.

Three

BEYOND THE VILLAGE

For the first part of my life I knew the village, my family, the Nile and the animals around it, and almost nothing else. I didn't know of the war, because that was something that happened in *madina*s – cities or towns – not villages, like mine. Then the war grew and moved, and strange, unfathomable things started happening, one after another.

First came a convoy of rumbling vehicles. I had seen a vehicle before – a man in the village had once used a large vehicle that was all wheels and seat to plough a field. I didn't know that there was more than one vehicle in the world, though, let alone all these trucks, bouncing along on the hardened mud.

Alongside these vehicles were men wearing cloth on their bodies and legs. I'd never seen that before, either. To add to my confusion, these men had lighter skin than the people of the village, and they all held shiny sticks.

I was intrigued but also scared of these men and their vehicles and shiny sticks. The men sang songs that I didn't understand. I later found out that the songs were fierce, about a powerful god called Allah, whom I suspected could not be eaten.

Of all my brothers, perhaps the closest to me then was a fully grown man named Adut. Despite the age difference, we were particularly close because he and I shared the curse of stammering.

I asked Adut about the men I had seen down at the river banks and he looked at me as though he was trying to explain something very complex to me in simple terms.

'Th-th-th-there is a north, and i-i-i-it is bad,' Adut told me. 'Those men you saw, *they* are b-b-b-bad.'

I knew nothing of the north then. Initially, the men were exciting to me. They represented an adventure.

After I saw those men, Adut and some of the other men from the village disappeared, returning with strangers – familiar-looking strangers, but strangers nonetheless. These strangers had shiny sticks, too, and were always asking for food and water. They were blunt and abrupt about their needs, and I could tell they annoyed the mothers.

There was a collective name for these men and it was Anyanya, which literally translates into 'snake poison'. The Anyanya were fighters, but not fighters like the men who wrestled in my village for bragging rights or status, and not even the men who fought the Palek. These men were in a fight that made them harder, meaner, and gave them marks on their faces, and holes in their bodies.

Adut went off with these Anyanya once, and came back with a hole in his shoulder that made his arm all but useless. Then, one day, I saw my first machine of war. It was an old tank, which was sitting in one of my uncle's fields. It looked like a metal house, with a beak. I asked my uncle where he got such a thing and he said that he and the Anyanya had killed the men in it and dragged it to the village. I asked if the tank was still alive, but he said it wasn't.

I wondered what my uncle would do with this metal house. My answer came some weeks later when I saw people working in the fields with new metal hoes, shovels and rakes, some bearing markings unique to the tank, and some still bearing the burn marks from the Anyanya attack.

The signs of war came before the danger.

When the danger first came, it came in the form of a realised myth. I had always thought the story of the *nyanjuan* – female werewolves who feasted on children – was a fiction made up by adults to keep their little ones from venturing too far into the bush, but when my cousin Makaroau Deng was attacked by one, I knew they were real. Deng escaped with just facial injuries, but when he described the attack later, it was obviously the work of a *nyanjuan*.

I soon saw the *nyanjuan* with my own eyes, prowling around on the edge of the village. They looked just like hyenas, but their eyes were wilder, and their growls were evil, and I could tell that they were far more dangerous than hyenas.

Of course I now know that there is no such thing as a *nyanjuan*. I now know that what I saw were just hyenas turned desperate – their feeding patterns interrupted by the bombs and guns. They had resorted to eating the dead bodies nearby, and sometimes tried to attack children like Makaroau Deng.

The Anyanya came to the village more and more as the war expanded. We fed them, and housed them, and let them rest when they had holes in their bodies or when they were sick. Other men from the north also came closer to us.

There was a missionary school in the nearby town of Mading, which hosted people who were teaching writing and reading in a language called English. If you could read this language then you could read a powerful magic book called the Bible. The men from the north hated that book, the language and the town.

One of my older brothers, John, went to Mading and learnt about the Bible. He had not been born with the name John, but the people who taught him about that magic book told him he had to take a name from the book and get rid of his old name. His old name was Bench Mach, which means 'god of fire'. His new name was the name of one of the men who wrote the Bible.

John used to tell me about the stories in the magic book, but they sounded unbelievable to me. I told John that his god didn't know much about life on the Nile. That used to make John very angry.

There were a number of times that John's religion put him at odds with many of the rest of us. There was one instance when, after learning about some things called 'graven images', he decided he was going to burn some of the wooden statues of our Dinka gods.

The mothers were very upset with John's vandalism, but people in the village generally did not mind the

Christians like John, and understood that they did strange things sometimes.

People were inquisitive about John's god. This was a god who claimed to have powers like lightning, summoning and resurrection. The people in the village reasoned that they might need his help against the encroaching Arabs from the north.

John said that his god had told him he had to go away to fight the Arabs, so he left the village with another of my brothers, Adut Malieth. When I asked people where they had gone, I was told they had gone away to become 'officers', which was confusing because John had told me they wanted to be soldiers.

One day the Arabs had a fight with the Anyanya near our village. When the fighting started, in between the sounds of roaring thunder I could hear a lot of yelling in a language I didn't understand. The fighting started in the day, and when the sun went down the fighting continued.

At night the fighting looked like nothing I had seen before. Lights, like stars but much brighter, flew backwards and forwards, with some of the lights flying across the river and over our village with a sound that was like breaking wood. My little cousins and I were so engaged with the show, we decided to move to a *luak* close to the river so we could get a better view.

When my birth mother found us, huddled near the river, eyes full of those tracers, shells and bullets, she yelled at us with a real fury. 'It is dangerous, you stupid boys!' she shouted at us. 'Do you want to be killed?'

I didn't move. I didn't know what it was to be killed, but I knew that I wanted to watch the show. After being dragged to safety, my buttocks were again whipped.

Four

OUR VILLAGE ATTACKED

For some time after the battle, the men from the north would come to our fields to burn our food and assault our women. Sometimes, however, there were long periods when the war was happening elsewhere. Sometimes it didn't seem that there was a war at all.

The only conflict I saw in those periods was the men who faced off in wrestling matches. That happened when one had questioned the other's manliness. I liked the wrestling. The men would fight with ferocity and then when one wrestler had forced the other to touch the ground, establishing himself as a greater man than the other, both would have to acknowledge the new order of things.

Even in the quiet times I remembered the war, though. Especially when I saw men in the village with holes in them. I always knew the war would be coming back, and I wondered what form it would take when it did.

I could never have imagined how it did in fact look. It was announced by my cousin – a deaf boy named Deng Yar, who was a little younger than me. One morning he broke the calm of the early hours by running around the village yelling, in mangled, consonant-less words, 'Beware, beware!'

He was pointing to the sky, but not to any partic-ular spot. He was pointing at the entire expanse of blue. We all looked up, but there was nothing to see. There was sky, and some clouds, but there were not even any birds to see . . . until there was a bird, but a very strange one. Most birds glide, like a fish in the water, but this one walked like a man in the middle of a long journey.

The not-bird came closer and closer. Some of the other children had gathered around us. None of us knew what this was in the sky, except, apparently, Deng Yar. He was wailing, agitated and scared, his hands jerking around, palms first, in an awkward dance of fear.

My adrenaline was rising, but I didn't run until the first bombs from the aeroplanes started landing. The bombs did not land close to me, but the sound of them shook my insides. Through the thunder and the fire and the smoke, frantic mothers collected their children and ran for the river, seeking the relative safety of the other side.

We were lucky; we had a canoe, but many had to swim across the river to the marshes on the other bank. We first watched the northerners attack the village from the sky, and then later we watched as they piled out of trucks and attacked us from the ground.

They shot their small guns and their big guns at the village and the marshes. There was metal and fire spitting at us, and it was chopping down the trees and the people.

Then, it all stopped.

Some of the villagers went back across the water immediately, and some waited hours, days or even weeks. The dead were buried and, for those who were not killed or wounded, life continued in the village more or less as it had before.

The northerners came back, though, time and time again. As we hid in the marshes, my cousins and brothers would try to figure out what the Arabs had come for. Did they want grain? Did they want our sheds? Had they come for the cows? Had they come for the river?

Eventually we figured that they wanted none of those things – they had just come to kill us.

I wished once again that it were possible to eat the big god *Nhialic*, not because I wanted to fill my belly, but because I wanted to get rid of the sky and the fire-bringing beasts that now lived there.

And then, one day, the northern army stopped having the run of our village. Their planes and trucks and men had fire and metal thrown at them by the Anyanya . . . only they *weren't* the Anyanya anymore, they had become something more dangerous, organised and effective. The Anyanya had joined a new army, which was now called the Sudanese People's Liberation Army (SPLA).

The SPLA was just as much of a burden on the village as the Anyanya had been, demanding food, shelter and medical help, but at least they were fighting the northerners with big guns and strong men.

Even through a child's eyes, I could tell that the SPLA was stronger. They had clothes that blended into the trees, and all the men fighting for the SPLA had guns. People started to wonder out loud if perhaps this army could stop the northerners.

But the SPLA was not strong enough to beat the northern army. Not yet, anyway. They were being equipped, funded and supported by the government of Ethiopia, which is a country to the east of Sudan, but they lacked the manpower to conduct effective offensives. Their thin ranks were being decimated by the airpower of the north, and often cut down by the inter-tribal conflict.

Many SPLA recruits had even been killed by the Anyanya as they tried to make it to the rebel bases across the border in Ethiopia, before the two armies decided they would fight on the same side.

The SPLA needed manpower, and they were going to get it from the only abundant source left in the country: the rural villages that were now populated mostly by women, the elderly and children.

It would be unthinkable to bring women into the war, and the elderly would not even last the journey to the SPLA bases, but the boy children could pull the trigger of an AK-47 almost as well as their uncles and fathers. They could be taught to become extremely loyal, also.

The fighting of this war was not only done on the battlefield, and those who needed to be killed were not just men carrying guns. The Sudanese People's Liberation Army would build an army of war boys. I would be a part of that army. I would be a war boy.

I remember how I spent my last day as a civilian – I played at being a man. I sat with our tame cow, which didn't go out to graze in the fields but stayed close to home to give milk. I pretended to own her, and gave her stern orders, which she acknowledged only with blank stares and defecation. My voice changed when I told her that one day I would probably have to give her over to another man, another man with a very fine daughter who would be strong enough to carry an antelope on each shoulder, and who would be so tall that she could touch the roof of a cattle shed just by reaching up.

I rubbed the cow's neck apologetically. There were more blank stares and more dropped poo. In the dirt at the cow's feet, I designed my own cattle camp. This was one of my favourite games – moulding clumps of wet dirt representing all the cows I hoped to own, penned in by a dirt fence, with twigs and sticks for the trees my cows would need for shade and a ditch dug with my heel representing the Nile.

When my camp was finished, I would move the mud cows around and imagine all the sons that would be working for me. I'd also compose the songs that would be written about my life – songs of hunting and fishing, wrestling and cow herding, songs about tall wives and strong sons.

There would be no songs for me, however, because that would be the last day I would spend in my village as a villager.

That was the day that I fell off the edge of the world of children and landed in another world. I did not land in the world of men, though – the world I yearned to be a part of – but another world.

In this new world there was no family, there were no gods, no Nile eagles and no *Nhialic*. In this world there was only one thing: the machine that is war. I was no longer Little Swallow, or the God Eater, and not even Deng Adut. I was SPLA. I would be that or I would be nothing.

On that day I was seven years old.

Five

LEAVING HOME

There had been fierce fighting the few days before I was taken from my village. The northern men had driven past the track next to the Nile in the morning, and when they returned in the afternoon they had been attacked.

After the battle, the SPLA came to the village – as they often did – to get food, goats and rest, but they were also coming to the chief with an instruction from their leader, Kuol Manyang Juuk, to gather at least one boy-child from each family.

The chief had no choice but to agree – our village was in SPLA territory now, and SPLA had guns.

The word went down to the clans, and then to the mothers. Athieu Akau Deng was told that she must give me up to the army. I don't know what the feeling may have been in her heart when she heard, but I believe inside she would have been collapsing.

It is a practical life, however, Sudanese village life, so knowing that there was no refusing the order, my mother of mothers started to prepare food for my trip.

Adut the stammerer was sent out to tell me to prepare for a long journey. I don't remember how I learnt that Adut was coming for me with bad news, but I definitely knew it, for I ran from him and hid in a tall tree with a great many leaves. I did not want to go on a journey, especially not a long one.

Adut and some of the other men searched through the afternoon and the night, but they couldn't find me. I came down from that tree at dawn, convincing myself that the danger had passed. Adut would have found some other boy to be sent off into the world.

He hadn't, though, and he caught up with me in the morning while I was playing with my little make-believe cattle camp. He approached me as one might a dog with pinned-back ears – walking slowly, leading with a gift of cloth in his hand. It was the gift that kept me from running away.

Adut told me that I had been selected to be educated. He told me I must go away from my mother for a while. He told me I would come back. He told me I had to be strong and that I would be going to

Ethiopia. I didn't know what Ethiopia was, but I knew my mother wouldn't be there and I didn't want to leave her.

The gift in Adut's hand was an army-issue khaki shirt.

I cried as he placed it around my shoulders.

'T-t-t-take this sh-sh-sh-shirt, and may you wear it p-p-p-proudly on the journey,' Adut said. 'Do you kn-kn-kn-know "proudly"?'

I did.

I had never worn any clothes before, let alone a fine khaki shirt like that. I left the shirt on my shoulders because I knew that I had no choice and would be going to this Ethiopia, no matter what my wishes were. There was no point in refusing the gift.

I was curious about being educated. I knew it was a great thing to be educated, but I hoped it didn't take very long.

While we prepared to leave the village, I found that I was not the only boy from my *luak* who had been selected to go away. My cousins Anyang Aluel, Adut Agor and Kueric Thuch – also tiny, crying and shivering with fear – would be travelling to Ethiopia too.

As the men waited to start the journey to Ethiopia, my mother held me one last time. She held me too long, though, and her fear started to seep into me.

I began to cry so she broke the embrace. The last touch I felt was her hand on mine as she gave me a parcel of sorghum, grain and nuts.

'You will have to be strong now, Little Swallow. You can no longer afford to be soft.'

There were thirty boys selected from my village – some a little older than me, some younger – and we were all marched, in one column, into the bush by some village elders. After a couple of hours of marching, I was as far from my birthplace as I'd ever been.

It was roughly twenty kilometres to Kolnyang, the first town we stopped in. I thought the journey was hard. I thought that my feet hurt, my stomach was empty and my mouth was dry. I had no idea how much worse things would become.

When we got to Kolnyang I saw two things my young eyes had never seen before. The first was a structure with a large tin roof, which made me wonder if Kolnyang was one of those things called a city that some of the Anyanya had spoken of. The second was the great expanse of people.

These people were spread far, further than the limits of the town and my eyes. Most of the people were boys – their eyes full of suspicion and fear, and tears, sitting or lying on the baked dirt – but there were also soldiers, who smoked and looked bored and tired and annoyed.

In Kolnyang most of the boys and men were Dinka – although not all were Dinka-Bor – but some were from different tribes. I could tell that by their faces, and their bodies, and the language they used. Due to this mix of tribes, I was more fearful of this town than the bush and its hungry animals. In my village, I rarely met anyone from another tribe.

We stayed overnight in Kolnyang, in a temporary camp with everyone else, but at the setting of the sun, no children's songs were sung. The only sound that could be heard was a muted whimpering.

I did not sleep, and I don't think anyone else did either, except of course the soldiers.

The crying got quieter as the moon rose, but the sound of the boys never totally went away. When I sat up in the middle of the night I saw that almost every pair of eyes around me was open. I knew what all the boys were looking at. They were looking at the stars. The mothers would not be sleeping that night, either. The stars were perhaps the last thing that could be shared by both the mothers and the boys.

I knew that my mother would be looking at those stars that night.

Six

THE RIBBON OF BOYS

At dawn the next morning the journey to Ethiopia started in earnest. Our group would not start to walk until the sun was high in the sky, however, as a great number of clans were sent on the path before us.

When we joined the march, there was a ribbon of boys and soldiers in front of us that stretched all the way to the horizon. After a few hours of walking, the ribbon stretched out behind us, too.

The first day in the ribbon of boys was the easiest. There was still food and water, and there were trees for shade sometimes, and the blisters on my feet were not yet leaking blood.

The soldiers had not yet become desperate and angry, and, in some of us, there was even a sense of awe at being part of something as massive as this horizon-spanning column. But that awe didn't last long.

One boy complained constantly on the trip. He was perhaps slightly older than me, and as we marched he was given the name Adhal Ayor, which means 'a child who is disrespectful of the elders'.

After every couple of hours of walking, Adhal Ayor would sit on the grass, only moving on when prompted by a soldier.

'If you fall behind, you will be left for the animals to fill their stomachs,' one of the SPLA soldiers told him.

We heard the sounds of lions as we walked, and I think the growls helped Adhal Ayor to find the strength to keep walking. I don't know whether Adhal Ayor made it all the way to Ethiopia, but I think it's likely he did not.

On the second day we walked from Kolnyang to a Dinka-Bor village called Ajageer, and on the third day we pressed on into Murle lands.

We knew the moment we crossed into Murle territory because whispers started to ripple up and down the line. A new level of fear started to spread – the fear of being taken.

The Murle were a tribe of expert guerilla fighters (fighters that were not part of a regular armed force and who were often politically motivated) and often raided our lands to steal those things that were most sacred to us – cattle, children, our food and our mothers.

Being in the ribbon of boys was bad, but at least there were cousins and uncles around us. We were not in our villages, but – for the time being – we had food and water. Who knew what happened to the boys who were stolen by the Murle?

For most of the boys their fear of the Murle had existed almost since birth. My fear of the Murle coalesced around a gunshot wound that one of my mothers had on her shoulder, from when she had been shot in one of the Murle's many raids.

The soldiers were constantly on edge as we walked. They kept their rifles at the ready and their eyes on the bush. Sometimes shots would echo from behind or ahead of us. Sometimes a ripple of chatter would come all the way to us, explaining the shots. Usually it was some soldiers hunting antelope, but sometimes it was not.

When the Murle attacked us, they came in groups of three or four. Knowing that a frontal attack was impossible, they shot their precious bullets only when they knew they would find a target, and then they would disappear again, like ghosts. There were many Murle attacks along the way.

I don't know if the Murle stole any of the boys on that journey, but I know some were killed. Soldiers were killed, too, but the column never slowed.

That night we stopped at a Murle town called Gummero that had been occupied by a garrison of SPLA fighters. We stopped for just a few hours – the last proper night's sleep was behind us – and no one managed to get any sleep in that town. The stories of kidnap and death kept us awake and alert.

The next day, like zombies, we once again travelled through wild Murle lands, and the next day after that. There were more shots, and more stories and more bodies. When we would stop at the end of each day I would experience moments of unconsciousness, but I'm not sure I ever achieved something that I previously would have called sleep.

We crossed a desert, which was something I'd never conceived of, let alone seen. I knew that the sky could be empty, but the land also? The land was full of trees and rivers and animals and people, as far as I knew, but it seemed there could be emptiness below the horizon also.

After a few hours in the desert there was only dirt and sand as far as the eye could see.

One of my great-uncles – Garang Kudhur, an experienced soldier from the Anyanya – told us that from that point on the only water that went anywhere was in a mouth, until we could see a body of fresh water in front of us. No matter what we heard from the line in front of us, or even if we saw a town, we must see this water with our own eyes before we could wash or cool down with water.

We trudged and trudged and trudged, and for hours we could see only desert and could hear only the sound of our feet, except for the occasional howl or wail from an animal. We received water only a couple of times a day, and then it was just a slug from a jerry can (a container for carrying water). Soon the jerry cans started to run dry and our ration became a tiny amount from the cap.

And then we were only given enough water to wet our tongues – just enough to stop your mouth from cracking and bleeding.

After a few days in the desert some of the older boys started to act in a way that would have normally been seen as mad. Some ate mud when they found it, and others fought to drink the urine that was expelled when another soldier or a boy stopped to take a leak.

The trek went on, everlasting. I lost all sense of time and place, and I even started to lose confidence in the belief that there would be an end to the march. The thirst, the sun boring into me, and the pain in my stomach and feet was the only reality I understood. The tiredness was as infinite as the view in front of me. The walk could not get any worse, and it would surely not get any better. It just was, and would forever be.

The boredom was finally broken when I collapsed on the path that had been trodden by the thousands of boys in front of me. I did not try to collapse, nor did I try not to, it's just what happened.

I lay there on the dirt as blistered feet trudged past my face. I was not the first boy who had fallen with fatigue, and in each instance the soldiers had done a quick assessment. Could the boy be compelled to stand and go on? Could the boy be carried until he regained his ability to walk on unassisted? If the answer to both questions was 'no', then the boy's fate was left to the compassion of the boys and soldiers behind him, and compassion was in short supply.

Most boys marched alongside members of their clan or family. If a fallen boy's clan or family decided that he was too far gone to be helped, then he was almost certainly not going to be picked up by strangers.

I was picked up and carried by one of my group – I do not know who. I was bouncing in and out of consciousness. We must have stopped to rest when

I was unconscious, because I remember waking as everyone lay quietly on the ground, and I remember waking again as they were preparing to move on.

I managed to walk on. I went back to the groove of endless sun and pain.

I don't know if it was something that had always been planned, or if it was because too many boys were being left behind, but at some point in the desert march a water truck was sent along the line. Jerry cans were filled, but they soon became empty again.

I started to think that there might be an end to the trip when I saw a huge, shimmering expanse of water ahead on the horizon. For hours we marched towards it, but it seemed no matter how many steps we put under us, we weren't getting any closer to that water.

It was an effort to speak, but I asked one of the soldiers how far he thought we were to that water. It was the only question that was answered on that journey.

'Not water. It's a trick of the eyes,' he croaked.

I cursed my eyes. There was no water in front of us, but mercifully, after a few more hours, the terrain changed. We had reached the border.

Seven

ETHIOPIA

When we finally crossed into Ethiopia there were green trees, and animals and grass, and a wide, very welcome river. I now know that that river was never far from where we were forced to march. There were boys who were left behind unnecessarily. I do not know why.

Our first stop in Ethiopia was in a border town called Pachella – a beautiful settlement on the banks of the Blue Nile, which we couldn't enjoy at all. We were as fearful in Pachella as we had been in the Murle towns, because here we saw men with light skin, and the only light-skinned men we'd seen before had come to our villages to fight.

In Pachella we were given our first military rations. Soldiers with giant bags of corn came around each camp, handing out food. For us boys, they counted out the individual kernels of corn as they put them in our hands.

We stayed in Pachella for some days. Ethiopian soldiers and the SPLA had occupied the town, but they had no control of the road ahead.

There were Murle on the road, as well as Anuak, the people of the lands we were in, both of which had been known to attack SPLA patrols to steal their guns and ammunition.

There was also the threat of northern planes and helicopters. If spies told the northerners about a cluster of boys and soldiers on that road, bombs would have been dropped.

Eventually we were moved on to the road, and it was a long one. We were given small amounts of corn and water along the way, but we were not going to make it unless we found more food ourselves. Some Anuak tribesmen traded food – a grain-mash that was a by-product of brewing beer – on the line, and we bought it with what we had: in my case, the khaki shirt that my brother had given to me when we started the journey.

I was once again naked, but now many hundreds of miles from my village.

Eventually we stopped at a wooded area close to a river. This was Pinyudo, a camp that we boys would help build, and a place that a generation of southern Sudanese boys would either pass through, or die in.

For the rest of the world, Pinyudo was (and still is) a refugee camp, but for those of us there at its inception, the camp was a holding pen for boys, a place where we'd learn to become soldiers.

The first few months in Pinyudo were dedicated to building grass tents, cutting bush, and clearing paths and roads. My sole role in life then was hauling water from the river to the camp. It was months of monotony. My feet flattened a path from the camp to the river, and the jerry cans carved an odd-looking bald spot on the top of my head where they spent most of the journey from the river back to the camp.

Those were empty days.

There was no play, no fun, no movement, no purpose, and certainly no songs. All I did was try to keep up with the water deliveries, and get some food into my belly when I could. Some days I did not manage it, as the food was often stolen by the older boys.

I left my village fat and with a khaki shirt around my shoulders. Now I was naked, thin and quite fragile.

Sicknesses like measles, tuberculosis, whooping cough and chickenpox swept through the camp in waves. Eventually one of these fever-inducing diseases cut me down.

My journeys from the river became slower and slower, and soon I couldn't eat and could barely even drink. My skin got hotter and hotter and eventually I couldn't get up and leave my tent. In keeping with the conventional bush remedy for fever, I was placed in a corn sack and left outside in the sun.

The days went by and I only got sicker and more feverish until one of the soldiers dragged me to one of the larger grass huts, which served as a field hospital.

There were dozens of boys in sacks in that 'hospital', including my cousin Anyang Aluel, who was taken from my *luak* with me. We would look at each other, when we had the strength, and nod an acknowledgement across the hut. Anyang, like me, had gone through a transformation. His belly had shrunk and his cheeks had become shallow, and most of the time his eyes stared straight ahead as though he was thinking about something very large.

Yar Deng, one of the few women in the camp, and a relative of mine, treated my cousin and me with small portions of porridge, and large needles. The needles I reeled from and the porridge I routinely vomited up.

Every day some of the boys in the hut died. When they did, thread and needles were produced, and the opening of their corn sack was sewn closed. These sacks were placed in a large hole nearby.

Perhaps thirty or forty boys were taken to the hut after that particular outbreak. As far as I could tell, only two regained health. I was one of them. Anyang Aluel was not.

I was only seven and had not previously understood that the people who were cut down by the bombs, the boys who were left in the desert, my father under his mound next to the *luak*, and now my cousin, were never, ever coming back to life.

The finality of death only occurred to me then. Death had been around me for months, but I had never really understood it until Anyang Aluel, whose life circumstances had been almost exactly the same as mine, died. I knew then that death was forever.

While I was recovering from my sickness, all of the boys were called to parade. Parades were not an unusual occurrence. We were often called into formation, and then yelled at in Arabic for an hour or two by an officer, before having someone explain to us what the yelling was all about. This parade, however, would not be like the others.

44

From the time we got to Pinyudo, almost all of us boys had been overseen by soldiers and older boys, or even extended family, from our own clan. The sub-camps that had been established were largely similar, with all of the boys with me being Dinka-Bor and speaking the same language.

Now, however, this parade mixed up the boys. After the parade – we were told – no two boys from one clan should put their shoulders together. This was the rule, and breaking the rule would result in harsh punishment.

I suspect the reason for this move was to make sure that the boys who knew each other didn't band together and fight for better conditions.

Disease and malnutrition were killing many of the younger and weaker boys, and the older boys and soldiers mourned their brothers and cousins, and perhaps also saw a future where their strength might fail them, too.

After the mixing parade, my brother John, who had been ordered to the camp from the front lines, sought me out. John and I had not seen each other since I had been taken from our village, and I was surprised that he recognised me – small, sick and shivering as I was.

At seventeen, John was a veteran, even though he would barely be considered a man anywhere else in the world. He had been fighting in the war for some years, and had more than once been left for dead after being seriously injured by bullets and artillery.

I was very happy to see him. In John I saw a larger world than the small, awful world I was living in. Brothers were not supposed to be brothers that day, though, and John and I only had a few moments together before he was barked away by another SPLA officer. In the time that we did have together, John took off his shirt – which was cotton, red and beautiful – and put it on me.

'Things are hard, Little Swallow, but you will survive in this shirt,' he said. 'It will protect you from being sick, and from being hungry.'

This protective shirt was the second piece of clothing I'd ever worn. Perhaps it worked, too, because for the time I wore it I was neither sick nor hungry . . . even though that period of time was only a few minutes. For, as I was walking over to report at my new camp, a fist crashed into the back of my head, and then some feet kicked into my stomach. I was robbed of my only possession, and walked to my new home naked.

Eight

LOSING MY MIND

I was soon reporting to an older boy of perhaps thirteen or fourteen, named James Mading Mabil. As was the case with many of the teenagers who were in command of a group of younger boys, James Mading Mabil was sometimes cruel.

Nearly every day after that mixing parade, I woke up soaked in my own urine. When James Mading Mabil found me sticky or smelling foul, he wouldn't beat me – he would order the police to do it. There were boy police just like there were boy soldiers.

For many months I spoke to no one except with a grunt or a nod. I was no longer near my relatives and I was sick and hungry every day. My only activity was hauling jerry cans of water from the river to the camp – an activity that would soon strike me mute with fear, as I knew that dropping the water would mean a beating from James Mading Mabil.

In these terrible conditions, it was only a matter of time before my mental health deteriorated.

One day we were called to parade. Once we were settled and at attention, a great number of soldiers – far more than I'd ever seen at parade before – walked in, with most fanned around one man who was obviously more important than all of the others put together. The man wore a military uniform and cap, and he had eyes that were set close together, which made him look very thoughtful, and a wide mouth that was framed by a well-kept chin-strap beard. This man was Dr John Garang, the leader of the SPLA and the father of South Sudanese independence.

When Dr Garang was seated, some of the older and fatter soldiers took turns giving speeches. When there were pauses in the speeches we would all clap and cheer enthusiastically, even though many of us didn't know what was being said. Some of the older soldiers led us in war songs, most of which I knew. I sang them as loudly as I could, as I knew James Mading Mabil would be watching.

Then, flanked by some fat SPLA soldiers whose uniforms I didn't recognise, some men were marched in, blindfolded and bound, and – in front of us – shot dead.

The horror of the situation made my legs move without any order from my brain. They were not taking me anywhere specific, they were just taking me away from what I had seen. My feet slapped on the ground and I heard the heaving of my breath. I heard shouting behind me. Another boy, perhaps a year or two older than me, ran past in a panic, and then another. They had responded as I had.

The last boy to overtake me was wearing shoes made out of old truck tyre rubber held together with nails, one of which he lost while running. I barely felt the pain as the nail of his shoe entered the arch of my foot. Blood poured onto the ground and dirt stuck to my foot.

I was limping by the time I was caught by James Mading Mabil. I expected to be beaten, but in that wretched moment Mabil's better angels took over. He took me back to the camp and treated my foot.

Each day I would examine the hole in my foot, looking for signs of healing, and every day I would find as much dirt and blood and pus as I'd found the day before. Then one day I found movement in the hole. Bugs called 'jiggers' – small, crawling animals like slimy, legless ants – had taken up in my wound.

I dug the jiggers out of my foot, but they had laid eggs, so there were always more whenever I looked.

Fever soon returned to my blood, and, with the pain in my foot, my thoughts soon could not be lined up properly. I started to lose my memory of words. I also started to have trouble remembering the route to the river, despite it being almost a straight line, and I forgot which bed was mine. For a time, I did not understand the correlation between the wetness I would wake up in each morning and the slaps and kicks I would receive during the day. I could not remember what was food and what wasn't.

There was more than one occasion when I was eating what I thought was food but it was actually human excrement that I had picked up from the ground.

I fought hard to keep the memory of my mother in my mind, though. She was my last link to my old life. All of the energy that was left in me was used remembering her name, and what her eyes looked like before I walked away from my village.

After a few weeks of fever, reality had almost completely escaped me. Most days when I woke, there was a haze on the plain just past the camp, and I could not escape the idea that it was the smoke of my uncle Gongich Ngueny Deng's cattle camp. When I saw that haze, I could taste the fresh milk he would be filling skins with, and the recently caught fish that he would be roasting. I thought I could eat and drink and get fat, like I had been, if I could just manage to get to that camp. Perhaps I could take milk to my mother and, with her guidance, I could get older? If only I could get to the smoke of Uncle Gongich's fire, I could perhaps have my own cattle camp.

I would run, limping but with gusto, for the haze, only to be dragged back by one of the older boys. Back at the tents, I would be beaten and told off. When the haze had dissipated, I would go about my water-bringing day, but the next morning, with the haze back, the mad routine would happen all over again.

Soon, to keep me from running away in the morning, I was tied to the bed each evening and only released when the sun was high in the sky.

Eventually my foot got better, but not my mind, nor my blood. In the mornings I would strain against the ropes until, as the fever rose and rose, I had no straining left in me. Eventually, I could not stand when ordered.

In those weeks I would have wasted to nothing except that my cousin Adut Agor took it upon himself to feed and bathe me. He had seen our cousin Anyang waste away to death, and he could not bear to see it happen again to his kin.

Adut would carry me around the camp on his back, and he was usually kind and compassionate to me, except that he complained about my jutting bones stabbing him in the back. He would take me to the hospital and try to get the nurses to fix me. Sometimes I would be allowed to lie down on one of the cot beds for a while, but they could never fix me.

I was Adut's burden for weeks and weeks. I shed even more weight, and my bones become as sharp as knives. My fever burned, I soiled myself whenever I managed to eat and drink, and I made no sense when I spoke. Yet Adut bore it all until, one day, while I was lying on a cot in the hospital, he said he had reached the end of his tether.

'Deng, I am not strong. Your bones stab me when I carry you, and my muscles ache at the end of the day. I have sores and sickness and we cannot go on. I think you are on the way into the ground.'

I knew he was right.

'We are all dead soon anyway, so we shouldn't suffer too much.'

My mind was everywhere, except where sense lived, but in that moment I understood what my cousin was telling me. I must die now. He must be free of me.

Considering how frail my mind and body were, I thought that I would be able to die by simply rolling off the camp cot. I tried to do just that, but I did not have the strength.

'You must help me,' I said to Adut.

He couldn't. Adut left me. I hoped he was coming back with a gun so I could die like the blindfolded men.

I waited for Adut and the gun. I waited and waited and waited, and night fell and day came, and night fell again, but Adut never came. I would have to stay alive. I would have to be a soldier and fight in the war.

I was nine years old.

Nine

A HISTORY OF SUDAN

When I was nine I knew nothing of the war, nor of the history of my nation. I only knew the lore of the Dinka. I knew that the Dinka world started when, one day, men emerged from the Nile with cows following them, as there is no world without milk, meat and dowry.

I knew that those early men used to go back to heaven via a long rope after they died, so *Nhialic* could fix their broken bodies and then send them back to their fields.

I knew that the rope was now gone, because a woman walked out of the Nile. One day when this woman was pounding grain, a baby bluebird tried to eat the grain. The woman killed the baby bluebird, and the mother bluebird, seeing her dead chick, chewed through the rope to heaven. In that moment, man became mortal.

That was the history that I knew, but it did not explain the war that I was thrust into. In fact, very few Dinka people believed that our history could explain this new war, so as the fighting dragged on people started to renounce the traditional history and align themselves with the Christian god that John worshipped.

Before the word 'Sudan' indicated a country, it was an Arabic saying and a loose geographical area. *Bilad as-Sudan* translates literally into 'Land of the Blacks', and is what conquering Arab military commanders called the area in Africa that sits just below the Sahara Desert.

Bilad as-Sudan was home to many African kingdoms over many centuries, but during the rise of the Ottoman Empire around the fifteenth century, Islamic rule was slowly established in the north of what is now the nation of Sudan. By the mid nineteenth century, Sudan's capital Khartoum and its surrounding cities were a mix of Nubian and Arabic cultures, but the south of the country, a fierce and underdeveloped area that is now the nation of South Sudan, remained largely immune to Arabisation and to Islam.

The north flourished in the Ottoman period until, in the late nineteenth century, harsh taxation policies and pressure from Europe to limit the lucrative slave trade encouraged dissent, which coalesced around a Messianic Islamic warrior priest named Muhammad Ahmad.

Using the fuel of powerful religious and nationalistic language, Ahmad built up a large flock of militiamen who supported him and, in 1881, proclaimed himself to be a Mahdi (a guided or enlightened one) and the true leader of the area known as Sudan.

The governance of the Mahdists was brutal. Beaten foes could either submit to the strictest interpretation of sharia law, or be put to death as apostates, which were people who refused to follow Mahdi's laws.

Once the Mahdi rebellion had successfully taken Khartoum, the Mahdi changed his title to *Khalifa*, which literally translates as successor or steward but also denotes a leader who rules with the approval of God.

The Mahdists proved a particularly efficient fighting force but, like most forces entering South Sudan, they won battles but didn't manage to influence or control the people. Still, their brutality spread and spread, even outside the nation's borders, with campaigns extending deep into Eritrea and Ethiopia.

Eventually, European forces defeated the Mahdi in the late 1890s. The great governments of the time were not particularly concerned with the fates of most of the east African colonies, but when a Mahdist army pushed deep into the continent-straddling nation of Egypt, a counter-offensive was ordered.

Historically, the story of the defeat of the Mahdi has been overshadowed by the enormity of World War I, but it should be noted that nearly one thousand New South Welshmen were committed to the defeat of the Mahdists as part of a British force. Eventually the Mahdists were toppled by a campaign headed by legendary British commander Lord H.H. Kitchener.

As a result, for the first half of the twentieth century the British – either directly or by proxy (someone else who would be acting on the British government's behalf) – ruled what is modern Sudan and South Sudan. For that period the nation was largely at peace, thanks in no small part to British recognition that Sudan was not one country but at least two, with the north being predominantly culturally Arabic and religiously Islamic, and the south being tribal, traditional and either Christian or animist.

Those two Sudans were ruled largely independently until, in 1946, the British decided that the two administrative regions should be merged.

Following World War II, the tensions between Sudan's north and south grew. While Britain's power and interest waned in the country, the north gained more and more power over the south, and the south lost government representation, consideration and the benefits of taxation.

Eventually things came to a head when, in 1955, the British prepared to give complete autonomy to a government which was increasingly run by, and for, Arabs, Muslims and northerners.

On 1 January 1956 Sudan gained independence from the British, and the new government instantly inherited a guerilla war that had started a few months earlier when a series of army bases in the south conducted mutinies.

For the first few years of what would eventually be called the First Sudanese Civil War, the southern fighters were largely disorganised and ineffective, thanks in no small part to internal tribal distrust and infighting – problems that to this day plague the nation of South Sudan.

The ineffectual war continued for some time until a Mahdi leader took command of the disparate groups of southern fighters and, for the most part, put them under a central command.

When that happened, the fighting was given another name, and that name was the Anyanya Rebellion.

After proving to be somewhat effective against the government forces, the Anyanya gained financial and material support from the enemies of the Sudanese government in Khartoum, including the country's largely Christian neighbour Ethiopia.

The Anyanya Rebellion lasted many years, and caused the deaths of hundreds of thousands of people from the south. The rebellion ended in 1972 when some very large Christian and Islamic groups brought the government and the Anyanya to a peace conference in Ethiopia's capital, Addis Ababa. The main concession offered to the south was that the southern part of the nation would be governed as one administrative district, with certain limited powers of self-determination.

When the peace agreement was signed, many former Anyanya field commanders voiced their concerns that the concessions agreed upon were too weak for peace to be maintained. Those commanders said that nothing short of independence would guarantee peace, and many kept their forces ready to commence fighting if need be.

This imperfect peace lasted until the early 1980s, when a block of Islamists gained political power in the capital and insisted that Sudan should be a wholly Islamic nation. The group ordained that the south should live under sharia law, with stoning and amputations legal punishments for anyone who disagreed with their law.

Khartoum, the capital of Sudan, dismantled the special autonomy laws that had been agreed upon, and seized the oilfields in the south that had been generating the bulk of the revenue bankrolling the south's limited independence.

The disgruntled Anyanya commanders reactivated their forces and the northern Sudanese army were also prepared to fight.

One southern colonel, who'd been absorbed into Khartoum's army after the end of the Anyanya Rebellion, planned a mutiny. That officer's name was Dr John Garang.

In 1983 Dr Garang – who was ethnically Dinka – had been sent by the Sudanese government in Khartoum to Bor, a Dinka town, to pacify a southern garrison on the verge of revolt. Instead, however, he killed the northern soldiers in the town and took the southern soldiers into the bush. There they were reformed as an anti-government force named the Sudanese People's Liberation Army, the SPLA.

With help from neighbouring Christian nations, the SPLA become an effective force. The Sudanese government was forced to the negotiating table, but this time the SPLA would accept nothing less than independence. In 1991 negotiations completely fell apart.

Both sides prepared for war.

The north prepared itself for a short, modern war, buying up fighter jets, bombers and helicopters. The south prepared itself for a long guerilla war, enacting general conscription, compulsory enrolment in the armed forces, and then scooping up boys like me from southern villages like mine, so they could be deployed against the northern soldiers.

It was a long and brutal war. When the fighting finally ceased it was estimated that roughly two million people had died, with most of those dying of starvation or disease.

Ten

PREPARING TO FIGHT

The camp at Pinyudo began to change. Women were brought to the camp for the first time, and girls, and *kawaja*, which is what we Dinka call white men. I had never seen any white men before. At first I was confused because I assumed they were Arabs, then I thought they were those lighter-skinned men from the SPLA that I had seen at the border, but they didn't act like either of those groups of men, and, besides, they were so white they were actually pink.

These white men brought food and medicine. They wore blue hats and came from a country called Australia. They fixed my fever, and soon I could walk, carry water and straighten out my thoughts.

There were all kinds of new food in the camp when the *kawaja* came, with the best being a type of wheat that we called *digigstralia* – a combination of the word *digig*, a local term for flour, and our best attempt at saying the word 'Australia', which was where the blue-hatted men said the food came from. We would mix that *digigstralia* with oil and cook it on hot metal plates. Even now, the thought makes my mouth water.

The blue-hatted men issued me with clothes – a pair of white shorts and a singlet. I wore that outfit proudly for at least a year. When my shorts developed holes in them I'd spend days hunting for scraps of cloth so I could patch them up. When there were lice in my clothes I'd spend hours baking them on the banks of the river in the searing sands to kill the parasites and their eggs.

I was proud of how I looked in my clothes, but they also had a functional purpose as, when stuffed with cardboard, they acted like armour against the beatings with sticks that I still suffered from the older boys from time to time.

This protection was especially necessary when an unknown disease that caused weeping welts on the buttocks swept through the camp. Bottoms were universally sore, and I remember one of the boys, who had been washing in the river, running screaming as fish began eating the exposed strips of his buttock flesh.

Things were still difficult then, but life was also easier than it had been before. Boys were still dying, but at a lesser rate. It was good to wear clothes and eat food. I started to remember who I was, and where I was from, and I started to remember that there had been people who had cared about me.

We started worshipping those *kawaja*, the white men, because they usually brought food, clothes, utensils or medicine with them when they came. The other boys and I would compose light-hearted children's songs – the first any of us had sung since we'd left our villages – about these magic people of abundance, and we'd sing them heartily when the white men came into the camp.

The SPLA were also happy when the *kawaja* came into the camp, but only if the soldiers had been tipped off before they came. Before the white men arrived, the soldiers had much to do: their uniforms had to be changed, their guns stowed, and the wooden training guns taken from the older boys.

I think that the SPLA accepted, and probably even helped, the UNHCR ostensibly taking control of the camp. The SPLA would lose fewer boys, and have far stronger boys when it came time for them to start their military training in earnest, with the agency's aid.

My military training really started when I was nine. One day when the *kawaja* were far from the camp, a group of boys my age were called to parade and there our heights were measured against an upright AK-47. Those, like me, who were taller than the gun were told that we were moving on from the camp.

I had been close to dying before the camp improved, so I was wary of a change of circumstances. But I also couldn't help but feel some excitement at what felt like a progression. Ironically, I had started to feel more like a soldier since the *kawaja* had come. The white men were outsiders – welcome outsiders, but outsiders nonetheless – and their world of food and clothes seemed less real than the world of parade, training with wooden guns and hearing about the glorious victories on the front line.

Camp life had seemed disorganised and random, but it had been effective because at the time when the SPLA needed me to start thinking like a soldier, I was doing just that. I enjoyed having a wooden gun in my hands, and I no longer hated parade. The discipline that had seemed so brutal started to feel comfortable to me. In fact, it started to feel necessary.

In the weeks before we were taken to our second camp I had started to think about the northern men who had come to our village. I now knew what death was, and I was starting to think about what it would be like to kill.

It was a two-hour march through the bush to our new camp, which was very different from the old one. When we had walked into Pinyudo there was nothing but bush, and even when we left there was little more than a collection of canvas tents, some wells and tracks and roads. When I arrived at the new camp, I marched into a military installation, with gates, ammunition dumps, machine-gun nests, barracks and firing ranges.

From the moment I stepped over the border of that camp I was very much an SPLA soldier.

We were taken to a barracks and placed under the command of a squad leader. Each squad, which was made up of ten boys, was assigned two sister squads, which became a platoon. The platoons picked up four other platoons to make a brigade.

From the moment we walked through the gate it was drilled into us that our squad mates, our platoon mates and our brigade mates were now the most important people in our lives. My brigade was my new tribe, the boys of my platoon were my extended family, and my squad mates were my new brothers.

There would be replacements for my mother and father, too, which would be my rifle, the AK-47, and Dr John Garang. Nothing would be more important to me in my life than my rifle and my leader – that was drilled into me every day of my training.

For months I had trained with a wooden gun, and I dreamed of the day when I would have my own rifle, with the power to fight and kill, and fulfil my purpose designed by my leader. Without the direction of Dr John Garang I was listless, and without my weapon I was ineffective. With one in my heart and the other in my hands, there was no limit to what I could do.

My unit was called the *kamanch* (claw hammer) brigade, under commanding officer Paul Ring Dau. Dau was my link to the wisdom of Dr John Garang, which would filter down via the brigade leader, then the platoon leader and finally my squad leader.

The discipline in that military camp was extreme and violent, but it worked because our leaders had started to establish purpose. Almost every boy accepted the way things now were. For those who didn't, they would most likely not survive. Executions were a regular occurrence. Every day in that camp the war seemed to come closer to us, and in war, you fight and take orders or you die.

In that camp we slowly but surely became effective, faithful killers.

One day we were called to parade, and a group of older boys marched in front of us before being deployed to the front lines. To see them, firm and stoic, carrying the weapons that they would soon use, made us burn with jealousy. Being issued an AK-47, and then sent off to a place where there was an endless supply of northern men to kill, was what every boy in the camp wanted. My only consolation for seeing those boys was that I knew one day I would be joining them in glorious battle.

Eleven

AN ATTACK

We would have to wait much longer than any of us expected, though. Unbeknownst to us boys, there was another war raging nearby.

It happened one evening when we were confined to barracks. We had been hearing gunfire outside the wire for some days, and that night the staccato *rat-a-tat-a-tat* was being joined by the deep booming of artillery landing nearby.

We lay on our cots with our eyes open as the barracks roof shook from the bombs. I had no idea who was doing the shooting, or why, but we could tell that the officers were becoming increasingly agitated as the explosions sounded closer and closer to the camp.

Then the call came. The platoon commanders rushed into the barracks and told us to evacuate. There was no plan for escape; we should just grab what we could hold in our hands and run when there was a break in the shooting.

When I got out of the camp I could see tracer fire overhead, and the flash of artillery explosions illuminating the night. Boys ran in all directions, but we mostly ran west, towards Sudan.

I know now that the forces that nearly overran our camp were from Eritrea, a country to the east of Sudan. The Eritreans were fighting for independence from Ethiopia. As we were allies of the Ethiopian government, the Eritreans were not on our side.

I ran through the night towards the border. When I got to the banks of the Gilo River, the rough border mark between the two countries, I encountered a crowd of frantic boys looking backwards and forwards, trying to choose between two terrible fates. In front of them lay a black blanket of water, rushing, peaking and roaring a terrible roar. Behind were the Eritrean troops, giving chase and firing at us.

Despite being a fisherman's son who had lived on the Nile, I, like most of the boys, had not learnt to swim. John had tried to teach me just before I was taken into the army, but I had slipped from his grip while he was spurring me to kick my feet, and ended up sinking. It took him quite a few moments to find me again, and not before I had roiled and rolled underneath the canopy of the Nile and developed a hatred of being underwater.

A rope had been strung across the Gilo to help the boys cross, but it had broken, sending some of the boys under the dark, wet surface. Some emerged and made it to the bank. Some didn't. A second rope was being strung, but the sound of gunfire was getting closer and closer.

When I entered the river I clamped both hands on the rope, gripping tightly with fear. It was only adrenaline that allowed me to let go with my rear hand and hold on with my front hand.

By the time I got to the Sudanese side of the river, I looked back to see that the Eritreans were fighting the SPLA rearguard, and the boys who couldn't swim had thrown themselves into the river anyway and were flailing around. When there were no more Sudanese on the Ethiopian side of the Gilo, the Eritreans stopped firing and started screaming at us in Arabic.

We stopped and stared. In the moonlight I saw that the advancing troops were mostly women, and that they were flashing their private parts at us. I later learnt that women comprised about one third of soldiers from the Eritrean People's Liberation Front.

We retreated into Sudan before these mad women could follow us. The structure of our units had broken down. Some went south, but most of us went west, retracing our steps to Pachella, where a refugee camp had been established.

When I entered that camp I became, for the first time in my life, a legitimate refugee and found that a refugee's life was indistinguishable from that of a soldier-in-waiting. The months after fleeing Ethiopia were very lean indeed.

There were no *kawaja* in blue hats, and no *digigstralia* in the camp at Pachella. Most of us survived on whatever bush fruit we could scavenge. Once again us boys became thin and sickly, especially the boys who ate the wrong fruits. More started to die.

Then, one day, planes flew over the camp and threw cargo at us. Too weak to run from the planes, we just watched the shapes float down towards us. We were happy to find that the cargo didn't explode, and ecstatic to discover that it was crates of wheat and medicine. The wheat was not *digigstralia,* but we were in no position to be picky.

I gained some of my bulk back when the *kawaja* started dropping food into the Pachella camp, and then lost it all again when disease swept through the camp and my fever and weakness returned.

At the height of my sickness, when I was wondering if I would survive, I was placed in a small plane and flown to a military hospital in a South Sudanese town called Kapoeta. There I received treatment. I can only assume that it was a family member in the higher ranks of the SPLA who managed my transfer, but I have never been able to identify whom it was that arranged that flight. I suspect I owe my life to him.

Even though Kapoeta was in a fertile part of the country, and on the Singaita River, the town looked like a desert. All of the trees near and in the city had been destroyed by fire or design, so there was no cover for anyone trying to attack or defend. A town of great strategic importance, Kapoeta had been taken and retaken a number of times already during the war, so everyone in the town was on tenterhooks.

When I had recovered from my sickness I was moved from a hospital to military barracks in Kapoeta. I learnt that, shortly after I had been airlifted out of Pachella, planes and helicopters from the northern-controlled government bombed the refugee camp and then seized the town.

After a couple of weeks in the crowded barracks, government planes started to arrive at Kapoeta. Amid heavy bombing, we fled that town. Shortly after, it once again fell to the government, with many deaths on both sides.

After Kapoeta we walked through the bush to a town called Kedipo, and there my brother John once again crossed my path. The SPLA were attempting to take Juba, the largest city in the south, and John, then a radio operator, was to be part of a bolstering force.

John was stunned to see that I was still alive. He had heard that I'd been killed. We only spoke for a short while, each explaining how the war raged around us. Both of us had seen cousins on our travels, and both of us had seen them die.

We were both very sick. John had scars from bombs and bullets, and something poisonous had bitten his foot, making it balloon up to twice its normal size. We were alive, though, both of us. That fact seemed like a miracle.

'I hope to see you again, little Deng,' he said to me with as much tenderness as is possible for someone in the middle of a war. I remember watching him hobbling off, and I remember hoping that one day I would see him again.

The government bombers came to Kedipo shortly after that meeting with John, and it quickly became apparent that it too would fall to the Arabs. As far as we knew, there was only one more place to flee to: a town named Torit.

Twelve

TORIT AND AMEH

Torit was a town that the northerners hated perhaps more than any other. It was the home of the first Anyanya Rebellion in 1955, when southern soldiers turned on their Sudan Defence Force officers and disappeared into the bush. Furthermore, everyone knew that the famous and ferocious Kuol Manyang Juuk commanded the garrison at Torit. I had never met this man, but he was a relative of mine and, at the time, I was proud to be related to a man who had such a reputation.

Torit was a fertile town, with abundant mango, coconut and fig trees. Close to the border with Kenya, it also had no shortage of goods coming in and out. If the tide were ever to turn in the war, it felt to me it would happen in a town like Torit, and so we were happy to arrive there. But a few days after our arrival the town started being bombed with a ferocity I'd not seen before.

Every day, giant Antonov An-24 and An-26 transport planes, heavy with crudely made barrel bombs, lumbered over the town before releasing their loads and soaring away, light and free. We would wait for the whistle, followed by the boom and the searing jagged metal.

I have a strong memory of one of the air raids – the second of that day. I was running with another man to a hole in the ground when a bomb landed close to us. The man's head was sheared off by shrapnel. The headless body seemed to keep running for some seconds before it fell limp into the mud. I suppose it must have been a trick of the mind.

Those were long, dangerous days in Torit. There was nowhere else to go, though, so we scavenged food, ran from bombs and hoped that the SPLA units elsewhere were making gains.

We heard bad things about the Juba offensive. People said that the government soldiers were repelling the attacking SPLA, and that a great number of our soldiers had been killed. Then I learnt, from a distant uncle also sheltering in Torit, that John had been killed in the fighting.

I was sad when I heard the news, but my sadness was mitigated by the fact that I didn't expect to live much longer anyway. With no protection from the planes, our numbers were slowly thinning and I assumed that we would all die from bombs, or the offensive that would surely come soon.

Then a group of new SPLA soldiers came to Torit – older soldiers, some quite fat. They started to organise for those of us boys remaining who had been trained in Pinyudo to trek to the nearby Imatong Mountains in Eastern Equatoria, a region of South Sudan.

We took what food we could scrounge and said our goodbyes to the old men and women we'd been sheltering with, and started off on another journey.

Some of our trip was on open plains, but some was through dense forest. The trip took us through areas controlled by the Toposa and Lotuko people – tribes that at that time were aligned with the northern-controlled government. Though we were being marched by armed and experienced soldiers, a number of boys and soldiers lost their lives in hit-and-run guerilla attacks. Some of the killings would have been politically or tribally motivated, but most were just gun robberies, with the soldiers losing their weapons, ammunition and lives when they dropped off the pack to urinate or rest.

Most of us boys survived the trip, which took several weeks, and we finally arrived at a tiny mountain town called Ameh, near the Ugandan border. We found it swollen by hundreds – perhaps thousands – of my fellow Dinka-Bor, who were living in a hastily made camp.

I wondered why so many of my people chose to be so far from the Nile, until I started to hear the stories. Thousands of people had died, it seemed, losing their lives on the blades of sharp tools or bludgeons. Our cows had been slaughtered, and the *luaks* and fields and dams had been burned or destroyed. This had all happened over just a few days, and now more than 100,000 of my people had abandoned their villages. Many of them were sheltering in Ameh, because it was one of the last places that my people felt safe.

I thought about my mother.

As I listened to more stories, I was told that it was not Arabs who had decimated my people, but ghosts – man- and boy-shaped apparitions with ash on their faces and death on their minds.

Of course it was not ghosts that actually did the killing. It was men and boys. It's always men and boys. The killers were part of a faction of the SPLA consisting mostly of people from the Nuer tribe, the second largest ethnic group in South Sudan after the Dinka. Most of the killers had been SPLA soldiers who had mutinied when Nuer officers called for Dr John Garang to be deposed and replaced with the well-liked Nuer commander Riek Machar. They were calling themselves the SPLA-Nasir, named after Machar's base town, with their shock forces being a group of older Nuer boys who called themselves the 'White Army'. It was this last force that had enthusiastically conducted most of the massacres in and near my village.

Many of the White Army were killing my people to help fulfil a prophecy foretold by a nineteenth-century Nuer prophet, Ngundeng Bong. Ngundeng Bong claimed that a left-handed man would take over the world, and Riek Machar's spiritual advisor, a man named Wurnyang, was convinced that Machar was that left-handed man. The conquering of the world was to start with a massacre near my village.

In the weeks that followed, more and more scattered war boys were delivered to Ameh. They had come from throughout the south, with some walking for months. When it looked like no more boys were coming, we were all brought together for one last journey before joining the fight.

Like most of the boys at that stage, I was more than ready to report for duty. We had been homeless for so long; we'd been hunted and bombed and chased from town to town. We'd seen small massacres and heard of very large ones. Now we thought we had an opportunity to have our voices heard.

We all missed our mothers and fathers – not the woman and man who had made our lives possible, but the steel and the leader that would make our enemies' deaths possible. We were ready to kill.

Thirteen

CLOSER TO WAR

From Ameh we were marched to a garrison town named Moli, and into a military base like the one in Ethiopia. There we were assigned new squads. All of us boys from broken units around the south were now reconstituted as the Red Army.

I was ready to learn to fight and kill in that base, but for some reason it was not to be. I don't know why, but we were left in Moli without weapons or training.

As was seemingly the case for any camp where we were left to stagnate, parasites and disease ran rampant. Jiggers were everywhere, and some of the boys ended up permanently crippled after the creatures made their way deep into their bodies via a wound or orifice. One boy in my unit lost his penis after a colony of jiggers set up camp in his urethra.

Once again I was living in a familiar misery. The only framework of our day was military discipline and disgusting, meagre rations.

It seemed the camp was in disarray due to the Dinka–Nuer split, which was decimating the SPLA. Government forces routinely attacked the supply lines from the fields near the Nile to the mountain bases, but sometimes there were no supplies to transport anyway, as the civil war within a civil war also ended up killing farmers or pushing them from their lands.

In Moli we were given a handful of rotting sorghum grains each day, but they were not fit for a dog to eat. The grains could only be eaten after they were boiled in water flavoured with bush herbs. They did more harm than good. Almost every boy got sick after each meal, with most of us becoming severely constipated. Some boys got so sick they were taken to the field hospital.

In Moli there were both Dinka and Nuer conscripts in the camp, and there was no apparent disharmony between us until, one day, gunfire erupted. I don't know what prompted the fighting, but after the shooting finished most of the Nuer recruits disappeared into the bush.

From that moment, those boys, many of whom I had shared the long journey from Pinyudo to Moli with, became my enemy. The war between Dinka and Nuer was to intensify in 1992. Nuer commanders tried to turn the untrained boys into a guerilla force capable of attacking SPLA bases in the mountains. But the handful of green boys were no match for the hardened soldiers, and the wannabe Nuer commandos were almost all slaughtered.

They were my enemy, but I couldn't help but feel sad every time I heard of the death of a Nuer boy. As the war within a war worsened, conditions at Moli deteriorated. Even the hated sorghum became scarce, and there were often overlapping outbreaks of disease. Soon more than a dozen boys were dying every day. As a fighting unit, the losses were making us combat-ineffective without us ever having faced the real enemy.

The SPLA recognised this fact, so everyone who was able to was marched higher into the mountain range, to a town called Chukudum, which was now the centre of SPLA operations. While northern forces occupied Juba, Chukudum would be the capital of free South Sudan.

When we walked into Chukudum, we got a sense of how fragile the rebellion had become. There was a strong military presence – soldiers, tanks and other vehicles of war – but it didn't have a sense of permanence. Even Dr John Garang's headquarters comprised only a slightly larger tent than the rest.

The SPLA had chosen Chukudum as its base because it was remote and easily defensible, but also because of the turbulence created by the mountains nearby, which meant bombers couldn't have complete free rein over the area. Bombs still fell, but rarely where they were directed.

In this mountain base, Dr John Garang hatched a plan to turn the war around. The government had made gains too quickly, and to garrison every town they had seized would have required an army much larger than the one the SPLA had. They figured those towns could be retaken, and if they took them around April or May they wouldn't need to defend them because the ensuing months of rain would make it almost impossible for the government to move enough cavalry, artillery and troops to retake them. A large offensive was planned for strategically important towns.

While the south was a kingdom of mud, the SPLA would build defences, resupply from across the border, and establish militias consisting of local tribes. Dr Garang believed the course of the war could be turned around with a relatively small collection of shock troops deployed at the right time, along with the right tribal alliances in strategic towns. Torit and Kapoeta would be key, with those towns being the doorways to Uganda and Kenya respectively.

An essential part of the plan, however, was collecting the scattered soldiers-in-waiting like me from around the south, and getting them through intensive training so they could conduct these offensives.

For this plan to come into effect, there would have to be new, protected training camps in the hills. So, after a short stay in Chukudum, we were sent to a clearing which would become a training camp called Nattinger.

Once again I was making bush tents and carving out paths, but this time it was with purpose and urgency. As soon as the basic structures of the camp at Nattinger were erected, Dr John Garang visited us and spoke to us of the importance of our work.

As Dr Garang gave his speech, a group of fat, healthy soldiers in special uniforms eyed us boys up. These men were Dr Garang's personal bodyguards, and part of a dangerous special force known as the Bright Star Campaign (BSC, or Commandos). One set of BSC eyes landed on me while scanning the crowd, and stayed there. I met the man's gaze and was surprised to find familiarity. This man was a cousin of mine by the name of William Deng Malou Akau, whom I'd last seen in my mother's *luak*. He was one of the Anyanya fighters who had helped repel the Arabs who had come to attack my village. After Dr Garang's speech, he strode up to me.

'You have become big, Deng Athieu. Almost a man,' he said.

The food in Nattinger was a vast improvement on what we'd been given in Moli, but I was not that much bigger than I had been at age seven. I was taller, certainly, but not much bigger.

'You will be a soldier soon,' he continued.

'I hope so,' I said.

Then I experienced perhaps the first moment of happiness in some years when this cousin brought me over a full set of uniform khakis. I was too small for the uniform, but I would grow into it. I had never been so proud, and had never been so intent on fulfilling the promise of Dr John Garang's plans.

I would be a soldier. I would make my father happy, and I would also make my mother happy.

Fourteen

MY OWN RIFLE

I continued training for weeks with a wooden rifle until I was finally given the essential tools of a soldier: a unique SPLA number, the badges that would identify me as one of Dr Garang's fighters, and the most important tool any revolutionary needs, a selective automatic Kalashnikov 7.62 millimetre, gas-operated rifle, usually known as an AK-47.

Now I was ready to kill.

From when I first saw soldiers in my village as a very young boy, I'd known that the AK-47 meant power. From the moment I started training with the SPLA, I'd known that the rifle was an essential part of effective soldiering.

Once we started our live ammunition training, our conditions improved. Even then I knew that this was because our value was increasing. Every time we fired a round, the SPLA was investing in us.

Like the rest of the boys, I was terrified when I first pulled the trigger of my rifle. The shudder of recoil jolted my hands and almost dislocated my shoulder, the crack of the round escaping the barrel hurt my ears, and I was scared of having the bullet fly anywhere but the target in front of me. However, after a few weeks of live firing, I stopped being terrified and started feeling empowered. I started to believe that death only happened in front of our weapons. Behind me was only strength.

I had my rifle with me at all times. It was my life. I couldn't wait to point it at the enemy, depress the trigger and watch the Arab bodies fall.

Strangely, it was at that camp that I started to change my opinion of the Arabs, who we'd been schooled to believe were the enemy.

Just below our camp were barracks where captured northern fighters were kept. Collectively we called them Arabs, but most of them were Darfurian or Nubian, and many were just as dark-skinned as us.

You may think that the northerners would have been treated very poorly at that prisoner-of-war camp, but they weren't treated particularly differently from us boys – except that, at the end of the day, they were taken to their barracks and locked inside. They were fed, and they had water and rest, because they, like us, had a value.

In fact, perhaps they had more value than us, as many of them were skilled craftsmen, fashioning garments such as uniforms and ammunition pouches, as well as helping erect tents and barracks, and designing irrigation systems.

As we vigorously trained at Nattinger, those Arabs walked around the camp with their heads down, doing their jobs. When I saw their weakness, I became increasingly convinced that we were destined to become the warriors that Dr John Garang told us we would become.

It was only as I watched those Arab men – our enemy – that I considered what it would be like to kill the northern men. I thought about specific prisoners I'd seen, and what it would look like to line them up in my sights and watch them fall after I pressed the trigger. I decided that I had no desire to kill the Arabs in the camp, but that I would be capable of killing the enemy when the time came.

After a couple of months of training in Nattinger, word started to spread around the camp that we were about to be deployed.

I was convinced we were ready. We knew how to attack, we knew how to protect the flank, we knew how to shoot our rifles, and some people even knew how to use the big artillery guns. Some boys knew how to use the radio, and other boys knew how to put a bandage on another boy when he'd been shot.

As far as I was concerned, there was no more to know about making war. We were ready to fight.

Fifteen

READY TO FIGHT

Before we moved out there was a short ceremony and we were redesignated *Jaysh Azraq*, or the Blue Army – a new force that was tasked with taking back the small part of Eastern Equatoria close to the Kenyan border.

We were marched to a staging camp in the hills near the town of Kapoeta. Since I had fled it, the town had been subjected to heavy fighting. It had since been captured and recaptured many times over and was now occupied by government forces.

In the staging camp we were placed under the command of a man named Commander Majok Mach Aluong, and his adjutant Captain Luol.

Majok was perhaps forty years of age, which made him far older than most fighters in the base. Skinny and small, he had a narrow face which could sharpen even more when he found something he disliked. He was an intense authoritarian, but he was also well educated, and I immediately knew he had an innate sense of justice. I liked him a lot.

Captain Luol was a few years younger than Majok, and a much bigger man – certainly more than two metres tall – with broad shoulders, strong arms, and deep tribal scarring across his forehead. He was dynamic and fearsome.

The discipline at the camp was extreme but manageable, because the rules that we lived under were no longer designed to create subservient boys but powerful soldiers. Initially, morale under Majok and Luol was healthy.

Luol was a singer, and he would bring us together sometimes at the end of the day and sing verses of war songs to prepare us for the front line. The songs made us yearn for battle. All we wanted from life was to have a moment of heroism like the men in Captain Luol's songs. He sang with power and his voice would excite us.

Commander Majok would talk to us about what the virtues of a good soldier were. He would also tell us about the enemies that we could encounter in battle. It was not only Arabs who were our enemies, but cowardice. We must also be wary of the lesser tribes. They were not to be trusted, but sometimes must be cooperated with.

Knowing that we would be deployed near Kapoeta, Majok and Luol had decided to try to gain favour with the Toposa, a fierce, war-loving local tribe.

During the war, the Toposa were sometimes aligned with the SPLA and sometimes aligned with the government, depending on how the relationship could be turned into wheat or weapons. When the Toposa were aligned with us they would harass government troops and kill from within. When they were not, they were as terrifying as the Murle.

The Toposa had a hatred for an adjacent cattle-herding tribe called the Didinga. For generations they had been warring with the Didinga, usually over cattle grazing rights, but often over revenge for ancient slights.

The conflict had been particularly extreme since the mid-1970s, when the Didinga returned to Sudan from a decade of exile in Uganda. In Uganda, the tribe had been exposed to new forms of large-scale farming, and to education, which they now expected to have in South Sudan. The Toposa saw both things as a threat to the natural order of the area.

When the civil war came to the region, these tribal hatreds escalated. Understanding this well, Commander Majok sent word around the area that Toposa men could come to our base to receive grain and ammunition if they brought us the severed head of a Didinga tribesman.

The heads came in daily, and it was left to us boys to inspect them. When we found the tribal scarring and tooth extraction that denoted a Didinga man, we'd approve the distribution of a few clips of 7.62 millimetre ammunition or a bag of grain or wheat.

Bonds of brutality between the Toposa tribesmen and us were created in that base, and our leaders hoped these bonds would be useful to us when we reached the battlefield.

From that base above the front line, we boys took turns conducting patrols around the area. We relished those missions. We would be out in the bush, with our weapons, looking for spies or enemies; it was the closest thing we'd done yet to actual soldiering.

One day, six of us were sent out on patrol, and I was happy to find that an artilleryman a couple of years older than me, named Numeri, was one of our number. Numeri was a good friend. He was shorter than me, but very squat and powerful, and he was both a natural leader and someone who brought humour to the sometimes long, hot and arduous patrols. He could also get us to concentrate when that was called for, and he was the best at hunting out tasty bush foods when our stomachs grumbled.

Numeri had an especially acute eye for hives filled with honey. On this particular patrol he spotted a hive high in a tree, climbed up and had just brought his hand, covered with honey, up to his face when a single bullet from a sniper's rifle pierced his hand, nose and then brain. By the time he landed, he was already dead.

I scooped up Numeri's body and carried it back to the base. When Captain Luol saw this dead boy, he fell into a rage. He hollered that this was a Didinga revenge attack, and that the man who had killed one of ours needed to be found and brought to us. Even though we thought it unlikely that we would be able to find the Didinga sniper, we enthusiastically supported the idea of retaliation. Numeri was our friend. He had done no wrong. We also felt that the attack had been cowardly.

A few days later, in a moment of extreme good fortune or misfortune, depending on your perspective, one of our scouts spied a large group of Didinga tribespeople – most likely a family – moving past the base.

We were sent out to grab them. Although they were wary of us, they certainly had no idea of the danger we represented, because they neither ran nor put up a fight. Instead, they just let us take them into our camp. We interrogated them and beat them up, but even I knew that they knew nothing about Numeri and the sniper who killed him. The questioning and the beatings went on throughout the day and into the evening, until we were all tired and we went to the barracks to sleep.

By the end of the following day the Didinga people were dead. We had killed these people, but it didn't matter to me then.

There was so much death around, it did not matter how or why it came, nor even really to whom. If it were not *us* making the death, it would have been the Toposa, or the Nuer, or perhaps the government, or one of the sicknesses, or hunger.

Soon after, the SPLA ordered that our unit be sent to the bloody front line against the government soldiers in Kapoeta. It was what we boys had craved for years. But after the war, knowing just how few boys survived those front-line battles, I came to wonder whether the granting of our wishes wasn't in fact some kind of punishment.

I was eleven years old.

Sixteen

KAPOETA CALLING

Before we moved out for Kapoeta, a large group of recruits arrived. They were boys I recognised from Pinyudo. While the rest of us fled west to Sudan after crossing the Gilo River to avoid the Eritrean attack, these boys, led by some SPLA soldiers, fled south, ending up at a refugee camp called Kakuma in Kenya.

But the boys had heard the call of Dr John Garang – a song of rebellion and independence – and their ears had decided they needed to get closer to that music, so they left Kenya and returned to Sudan. They were our brothers.

We knew that they were with us when we heard their voices, full and strong, singing the war songs that Captain Luol taught us.

'*Walid jonub ma bicub yom chakel*,' Luol would sing. The sons of the south never fear on the day of the battle.

'*NAM! NAM!*' we would holler. YES! YES!

'*Ana reujjel chela ne mud, malu?*' We are men. If we die, so what?

Together we marched to a town called Lotouke. There we would be armed before being taken to the front line.

At Lotouke there were gifts waiting for us from nearby nations such as Uganda and Ethiopia. There was stack upon stack of AK-47 rifles, boxes of belt-fed machine guns, serpentine reams of long, sharp rounds, rocket launchers, and stocky mortars with their toy-like ammunition. There were trucks and Land Rovers, some of which had been opened with saws, like a can, so that the seats could be extracted and replaced with the larger guns. There were also giant CAT vehicles, which could transport troops across muddy roads on the fringes of the wet season.

The potency in these armaments and their explosive power made us feel strong. We had been training, so we were fierce; and we were boys, so we were rebellious. We had already seen death and no longer feared it, so we were also dangerous.

100

In Lotouke we all started to sleep with our weapons. At night I would caress the barrel and stock of my gun before dreaming of a time when my rifle and I could fulfil our destiny.

We started to hunt with our rifles, even though it was against the explicit orders of our superiors. We killed many of the four-legged animals of the area with the efficiency of hunters who had been trained to aim, anticipate and execute.

I was effective from about fifty or sixty metres when hunting with my weapon, but there was one twelve-year-old boy from my platoon, named Nyilo, who was lethal from a much greater distance.

I have never seen a shot like Nyilo. That boy seemed to have a supernatural ability to guide a round into a target, and he enjoyed the reputation his skill brought.

Once, when hunting in Lotouke, I killed a small antelope. As we skinned the animal, and made a fire, there was great praise for the shot, and many thanks for the meal we were preparing. Nyilo also praised my marksmanship, until he spied, off in the middle distance, a much larger beast.

'I will show you something now, Deng. The true marksman can kill without even leaving a wound.'

He fired two shots in quick succession, one that was fired high to scare the animal, and the second, only a heartbeat after the first, directly at the animal. It fell to the ground. We ran over to the catch, and the antelope was dead, as promised. There was no apparent wound, either, just as promised.

We asked in disbelief how Nyilo had killed magically, but he would not speak, holding only a knowing smile. The riddle was answered when blood started to leak from the animal's rear.

The first shot had caused the gazelle to turn from the shot, and the second had pierced the animal's anus as it tried to escape.

Our journey back to the camp was full of song – tales of death and courage. We expected to come into the camp as heroes, with meat enough for our whole platoon, but our Sergeant Major, Garang Akudum, intercepted what was meant to be a triumphal parade.

'WHAT DO I SEE?' he hollered.

The boys scattered, but I, who was heavy with a carcass, could not disappear so easily. Sergeant Major Akudum grabbed me and took me to a shed, where he brutally beat me.

All the boys hated Sergeant Major Akudum.

During the time we spent in Lotouke, we physically got no closer to the front, but mentally we inched nearer. We would show our fearsome intent by walking around the camp with the safety switch off our rifles, and a round in the chamber. This often resulted in boys accidentally shooting themselves, or their squad mates, so many of the boys – including me – ended up putting a round in the chamber with the trigger depressed, creating a deliberate jam that could not be perceived by the other soldiers we were trying to threaten. After all, it would have been sad to die so close to the front line without having fought.

When most of us left Lotouke we were marched to Kor Machi, the final SPLA staging base for the assault on Kapoeta. Our camp sat directly above the town, on a hill, and we could see our goal. It was the town I had run from while government bombs rained down, and a place of such strategic importance that I felt I would be honoured to die attacking it.

The towns of Kapoeta and Torit were doors to supporting nations Kenya and Uganda, and they were hallowed names for us at that point. Great, bloody battles had happened in those towns, battles that were immortalised in the songs of Captain Luol. As a western child might fantasise about Disneyland, we dreamed of Kapoeta.

We were so close to our dreams.

In Kor Machi, the older soldiers pored over miniatures of the town, while we waited for the green light to attack. Day and night, our artillery roared from a position behind us – death flying loudly towards Kapoeta. Day and night, mortars came in at us from the government positions below.

For the most part, their fire was inaccurate and ineffective, except in one instance.

That time, they used the smoke of a cooking fire to triangulate their target, and that round came in like an arrow to a bullseye, exploding right next to our cook while he tended to a stew. He was killed instantly, with his intestines leaping into his bubbling pot. There was an order issued afterwards that there would be no more cooking, and no more fires.

The skies were blue in the days before the assault, but our commanders knew that soon the clouds would come, and with them the rain. The movement of men and machines would be severely hampered then. If the SPLA were to take Kapoeta, it would have to happen very soon. Our commanders knew that, and the Arabs would have known it too. The upcoming fight could be felt in the air.

Seventeen

OUR FIRST RAID

After almost a week in Kor Machi, we were called to conduct our first raid. Our platoon commander, Manute Chin Ayuael, a man who had been training us since Nattinger, told us we were to take our positions.

'I have trained you very well,' he boomed, 'and I'm sure none of you will die before you have fulfilled your destiny.'

There were roars and cheers.

'Are you all ready to die?' he asked, with a glint in his eye.

'*NAM! NAM! NAM! NAM! NAM!*' Yes!

We repeated that word as we marched on Kapoeta. At a certain point in the bush, Captain Luol hissed that we should all shut up. We crouched and waited. We could see the buildings of the town below us, and we couldn't wait to be in combat. There was no fire coming in, nor any going out, but the thrumming in my chest was easily as powerful as any artillery.

We waited, crouched in long grass, for an eternity. Then we saw what we were waiting for – Bright Star Campaign (BSC) commandos. Strong, tall and with expressions of pure determination, they strode towards the town. My pounding heart nearly exploded when the sound of heavy machine guns and grenades filled the air. The battle had begun, and we were about to be called to join it.

Captain Luol and Commander Majok stood, and Majok turned to us with a smile of pure ecstasy.

'IT'S TIME,' he yelled.

Majok and Luol walked forward with an unhurried gait, and we followed in a low-profile crouch, as we'd been taught for such assaults. Soon we could see the buildings ahead, and the muzzle flashes from the machine-gun bunkers and sandbagged windows. Dirt spat at us as rounds came in, and trees splintered and flaked as they were hit by supersonic shards of metal.

Majok and Luol never flinched or slowed as they walked towards the town, even though tracers sometimes blasted, like lasers, between them. Majok and Luol had the poise of superheroes. The rounds continued to come in and I wondered if that pair of men could even be penetrated by something as mundane as a bullet.

As we moved ever closer to the town I could see that there were a number of fights already underway, with the BSC commandos engaging some of the machine-gun nests from cover.

We crawled on, and Majok and Luol strode on, and my heart kept thumping until Luol leaned back on his heels and hollered in an undulating and euphoric voice, *'HAJUM! HAJUM!'* Attack! Attack!

We had been waiting for the call, so we leapt up from our crouching positions and sprinted towards the town below. Guns that weren't already engaged turned to us and started to fire.

I often heard a whiz when a round made its way from Kapoeta, but every so often there was a crack, as though the bullet was shattering air. I will forever know the difference between rounds fired near me, and rounds fired at me.

We ran as fast as our legs could take us, screaming with bloody intent, zig-zagging in the way we had been trained to do. I could see the faces of the enemy now, those Arabic invaders who had come to our lands to steal our way of living, if not our lives.

None of them were of Arab descent, though – they were all Nubian or Darfurian, many probably press-ganged into the northern army, and all almost as black as I was.

But these men were still the enemy, and they were firing at us. When I was within effective range, I picked a window with a machine gun poking from it, planted my feet as I had been trained, raised my rifle and started to fulfil my destiny.

The rounds from my gun spat at the machine gunners with all the accuracy I could manage. The bullets in my clip disappeared quickly, so I advanced my position and, behind a tree, went down on one knee and popped in a second clip. *Cla-CLACK*.

My first mission was half over, as this raid was just an exploratory one. We were to sweep across enemy positions and expose the hidden machine-gun nests in the buildings and bunkers. When identified, the spotters behind us were to relay the firing positions to the artillerymen at Kor Machi.

When engaged, we were told not to dig in but to move on quickly across the battlefield. We were to be small and nimble, and judicious with what little ammunition we had.

I started running again and spent my second clip at another position that had opened up on our platoon. Soon my feet had thumped on enough dirt torn up by bullets and artillery that I was on the edge of the bush again, and protected from machine gun fire. I was out of range and safe. I could still hear the staccato chattering of enemy guns, but that song was no longer playing for me. My first battle was over, and far too quickly. Had I killed? I wasn't sure. Was I dead or wounded? After patting my body, I was sure I was not harmed. Was that really all there was to fighting in a war?

I came back from the battle with only snapshots of memory – far-away muzzle flashes, strained enemy faces, and the popping sound of guns. Was there nothing more for me than that? Was I more now than I had been this morning?

I dared myself to go back to the battle, to make sure that I hadn't missed anything. It had been drilled into us that a good soldier must forage in the battle-field, so I thought I would go back out into the field of fire and see if I could retrieve a weapon or some ammunition.

I snuck back in front of the guns. They were still firing, but I could tell by the sound of the fire around me that I was not yet in any gun's sights. The approach to Kapoeta was littered with bodies, but I couldn't see any weapons or ammunition to snatch. Eventually I decided to forage a second uniform, so I found a man roughly the same size as me whose deathblow – a packet of bullets to the chest – had destroyed his life, but not his khakis. I returned to Kor Machi with no further incident.

I wondered if I was now a soldier. I had the weapon, the uniform (two), and combat experience. I had fired at the enemy and had been fired upon. There was only one possible requirement that I most likely had not met, and that was the requirement of killing.

A smell followed me back to Kor Machi – a smell that first came into my nose in Pinyudo when those soldiers had been executed in front of me. It was the smell of death. Quite a large meal greeted our platoon that night, but I could not eat because each bite now tasted wrong. Food had been a joy of my childhood, and now it felt that my last possibility of pleasure had been consumed by battle. My hunger has never really returned, and even now I don't enjoy food like I once did.

As the artillery continued to rumble, we watched from our spot above the town, and waited for our second bite of combat. Each of us war boys planned, a thousand times, the path of destruction we would take when unleashed again. We had been too eager before, we agreed among us, and we'd also been too timid. Next time we would be methodical, efficient and ruthless. The enemy would not be so fortunate again.

With a head full of battle, I had three more nights of rest without sleep, and three more meals without hunger – that smell would not disappear – before it was time for our second attack.

Eighteen

THE SECOND ASSAULT

Our second assault on Kapoeta was to be a much larger attack. Four whole battalions were activated, and we were well supplied with clips of ammunition and grenades. Last time the plan had been just to engage the machine guns and then sweep left across the field of fire until we were out of range. This time we were told not to return unless Kapoeta had been taken. For our part, our unit was to advance with the rest and then sweep, as quickly as we could, to the flank, and engage the machine-gun nests there that would still be firing forward. It sounded wonderful to us.

We were called to combat at around midnight, and each platoon commander gave his troops their final instructions, and final words of inspiration.

'Are you ready to kill?' platoon commander Manute Chin Ayuael said over and over.

'*NAM!*' Of course we were.

'Are you ready to die?'

'*NAM!*'

'Not before you have killed, my men.'

Under the cover of darkness, we approached the town as silently as possible. It was to be a surprise attack, so we were to be attuned to every heavy footfall on the ground, every connection between rifle and buckle, every broken twig and branch. All I could hear was the pounding of my own heart.

We moved extremely slowly through the trees and shrubs on the same approach we had made a few days earlier. This time, though, there were hundreds of SPLA fighters to my left and right. The commanders motioned for us to stop. The darkness of night was still on us, and the attack would come with the first light of the day.

I stared hard at the sky, looking for the milk of the dawn. The thrum of my heart only got heavier. Fantasies ran through my head – of a battlefield littered with dead Arabs and the SPLA flag raised high above the buildings below us.

I looked at the boys around me. Their eyes were wild and wide, and they were unable to focus on anything for more than a moment. I was the same. As the black sky above us took on a tinge of purple, the commanders stood and motioned for us to move again, slowly and silently.

We had been well drilled, and no one rushed forward, or spoke, or coughed, or made a sound. We were just a deadly tide ready to drown the enemy occupying the town. In the pale light, I started to discern the machine-gun positions in front of us. I plotted my run down to the flank. I would have to move in a snake-like fashion to avoid being an easy target for the machine guns, if they were to open up. Perhaps they would not open up, though. Perhaps we could move close enough for our grenadiers to . . .

BOOOOOOM!

One of the boys in front of me was launched skyward by an anti-personnel mine. This was followed by enemy guns firing. By the time all of the machine guns were firing, the Arab mortars were landing. The machine guns cut many of the SPLA attackers down instantly, and straightaway a large number of us were trying to find a bunker or ditch. There was no cover, though. Majok and Luol stood fast and yelled for us to move up, and keep attacking.

Some SPLA machine guns opened up behind us and, with that suppressing fire at our backs, we tried to advance as ordered, but everything went from bad to worse very quickly.

The enemy mortars became more frequent and precise, lighting up the battlefield. The mortars brought with them concussion, heat and sound, which could be heard and felt, left and right, back and forward, and the approach to Kapoeta was soon littered with dead soldiers.

Majok and Luol were still standing fast, full of purpose, urging us to continue, but it was becoming physically impossible. A squad next to me was decimated when a shell landed in the middle of them.

Guns were cutting boys down to the left and to the right of me. When a machine-gun bullet hits you, you don't react, or fly backwards as you might expect – you just fall down.

A shell that landed some metres to my left blew me up into the air. I stayed intact, but the shrapnel punctured my head, groin and thigh.

Majok and Luol screamed at us to go on. They screamed and screamed and screamed, and I really tried to keep going. Bloody and confused, I ran towards the guns as best I could, but soon every step I took was into an explosion or direct gunfire.

Of the four battalions trying to assault the town, one had been pulverised by mines, one was mowed down by the machine guns and artillery, and another had fled (this battalion was made up exclusively of ethnically diverse conscripts, who were nowhere near as gung-ho as we were). That only left our battalion, which was at less than half strength after just a few minutes of battle.

Fire started coming in from our flanks – single, effective shots aimed at the heads of soldiers who'd managed to find cover. My comrades started to fall at the hand of these new snipers.

We tried to return fire. We tried to shoot at the snipers and the government troops, but we were now fighting on too many fronts.

Those from my brigade who were still able tried to wheel to the left flank as we'd been ordered, but the attack was over and we were just running away at that point.

I ran towards a tree beyond the range of the machine guns where I saw dozens of SPLA soldiers collecting. A man in my platoon, called Peter Raan-Dit, was running with me. 'You're bleeding,' Peter Raan-Dit said. Raan-Dit means 'big man' in Dinka.

My head was bleeding, and my body and legs were bleeding. I touched all of the spots where artillery had pierced me. None of the wounds had cut into the inside parts of me.

'No, here,' Peter said, pointing to the small of my back.

When I put my hand there, I found a gouge the size of a coin, and a faucet of blood pouring out. As soon as I felt the bullet wound, I fell to my knees.

'And here,' Raan-Dit said, pointing to my crotch. I grabbed my penis and testicles and found that I had been shot through the testicles.

I fell to the ground. I tried to stand, but fell again. Raan-Dit, who was strong and fit, for he worked as a runner, relaying information from unit to unit, hoisted me over his shoulder and pointed us towards the spot where the wounded were being collected.

From Raan-Dit's shoulder I surveyed the battle-field. It was a mess of torn-up dirt and torn-up men and boys.

Raan-Dit deposited me amidst a large group of injured and ran back to the battlefield.

A man who had suffered many gunshot wounds to the torso asked if we had anything we'd like him to tell God. Another man, who had lost a leg, said the man should tell God to make up a bed for him, because he would last longer than the other man, but not much longer. There was much laughter. I can't remember who died first, but both men were gone within the hour.

Raan-Dit came back again and again, always with another injured soldier and more stories, until he did not come back anymore, for he had been killed by the machine guns.

There was another SPLA offensive after ours, and that one was successful for a moment. The government machine gunners were killed, and their weapons were seized. Our attackers did not manage to take the enemy mortars, however, because the government troops mounted a counteroffensive, and our people were killed or driven back to Kor Machi.

Nineteen

THE AFTERMATH

In the days that followed, all the dead, including Captain Luol and Commander Majok, were left behind. No bodies were retrieved. It was not what was done in that war.

Eventually a truck arrived at our collection position, and us wounded were stacked in the back, like firewood. There were groans and shrieks as the wheels bounced and we were taken to Chukudum, where we were driven to a hospital for assessment. In that hospital, the full account of the battle could be seen and heard.

Combat triage was undertaken. Only those soldiers who had a chance of being returned to battle were being treated.

Even though I can feel my injuries to this very day, it was deemed that they would not preclude me from going back into the fight. My shrapnel wounds and the gaping hole in my testicles were stitched up, and a surgeon reached into the wound on my back and pulled out the largest part of the bullet. The smaller parts will perhaps be pulled out one day, but have not been yet.

More wounded arrived, and more, until every inch of every floor of that hospital was covered in wounded soldiers. Bodies were being carted out every few minutes – the dead or nearly dead – to make way for those who could potentially be re-used.

Eventually some of us were taken to trucks and driven to a town called Narus, close to the Kenyan border, and then over the border to Lokichogio. Although technically part of Kenya – one of the only countries in East Africa where there was no war at the time – there was war in Lokichogio, because the SPLA had brought it there. There were SPLA soldiers everywhere, and the hospital was full of soldiers who'd been wounded in battles in Eastern Equatoria.

I recovered for four weeks at that hospital. There was no bombing in Lokichogio, and there was food and water and also milk, fresh milk, just like the milk I used to drink at Uncle Gongich's cattle camp.

It would have been a good place to be, except that it smelled like death. I yearned to go back to the front line. I yearned to be out of hospital. There was no fear of death for us boys – we had been indoctrinated too well. I reflected on the assault. As it had started, a small part of me had feared that perhaps there was a lack of courage in me, but I had charged the machine guns, and could again.

I felt relieved when an SPLA man gave me orders to go back into Sudan. I still had problems walking, but I moved as confidently and strongly as I could, especially when in the presence of officers.

I was crammed into the back of a truck and driven across the border, eventually finding myself back at Nattinger. I hoped to be reunited with my unit but I found that there was no unit left to join. I was one of the few to find myself returned to service.

My new unit was called the *moakin*, or 'broken unit', partly because it was made up almost exclusively of soldiers from units that had been decimated in actions like the Kapoeta assault, and partly because almost all of us were wounded.

The tasks we undertook in Nattinger were menial and dull. We guarded prisoners, undertook reconnaissance patrols around the base, delivered bales of cloth and thread to the tailors making uniforms, and helped the mechanics fixing the vehicles that were going back to the front lines.

I desperately wanted to go back and fight. The misery of the work was compounded by the fact that I was still in pain every day, and I was suffering bout after bout of fever. We were very removed from the war we were all so invested in, except that sometimes we'd get a sense of morale rising or falling in the officers, or we'd hear battle stories from returned infantrymen.

There were months in this painful, sick purgatory, feeling like a ghost in Nattinger. Then my wounds miraculously started to improve, and soon my morale came back. 'Perhaps I will be able to fight again,' I thought.

I practised karate – a compulsory activity at most SPLA bases – and played long games of soccer. I started playing football with a boy of the same age as me, named Michael. Michael was not treated well in Nattinger because there were some rich people in his family and he, through their influence, had been able to avoid fighting in the war. I liked him, though, and not only because he was an exceptional soccer player. After games we used to share our experiences, and Michael told me about his sister, Elizabeth, who was across the border in Kenya and was married to an SPLA officer named John Mac, which was also my brother's name. This John Mac was from a village near Bor, and he was Dinka-Bor and the same age as my brother.

I told Michael stories of the war, and of my village, and he talked about this brother-in-law, who'd met Michael's sister in the Yita refugee camp in Unity state (one of the states of South Sudan) a few years earlier and then spent more time with her in Kapoeta, where Elizabeth was sheltering after fierce Eritrean women had chased her from a refugee camp in Ethiopia.

When John Mac saw Elizabeth in Kapoeta, he declared that he was going to marry her. A year later, Elizabeth was in a refugee camp in Ameh, near the Kenyan border, and another man was showing interest in marrying her. Hearing this, John Mac rushed to Ameh and married Elizabeth. He was then sent back to military duties in the town of Nimule, on the Ugandan border.

Michael was convinced that his brother-in-law was my brother. I knew better than to believe so easily; I had heard of my brother's death many times, and I knew that untruths were easily told during war, sometimes because of miscommunication and sometimes because of wishful thinking. I wouldn't give myself over to a hope.

Twenty

MY BROTHER LIVES

Michael took me to his mother's house and told me, in great confidence, that John Mac was coming from Nimule to pick up Michael and his other sisters and take them across the border to Kenya. This John Mac had also heard that his own brother was in Nattinger, and he would try to find him, too.

At the very least, I was convinced that Michael thought that my brother John was alive and coming to get us. I still did not completely believe, however, that it was a fact. Someone who was dead in the war was dead until you saw them alive with your own two eyes.

Then, one day, my brother John appeared. He was injured – with agitated, fissured skin, the result of an insect bite he'd suffered in Juba, and new scars – but he was very much alive. He also wore officer's stripes.

For many years I had believed that John had been killed in battle, and he had thought the same of me, so it was an emotional reunion. He had official dispensation from the army to drive to Kakuma in Kenya to receive more medical treatment for his wounds, and to take Elizabeth's family with him – Michael, and Michael's mother and sisters. John was expected to return to the war, but he had no intention of doing that.

In the never-ending spider-web of distrust that existed in the SPLA, friction between some elements of the ruling clique and the Dinka-Bor had emerged.

John spoke some English, and was better educated than many of the SPLA men – having learnt a little in the church at Mading near our village that the Arabs destroyed. Many of the uneducated officers in the SPLA were quick to draw assumptions about John's ambitions. In the SPLA, having ambition but lacking the guns to back it up was often a death sentence.

A small faction of powerful men, led by Dr John Garang's wayward son Mabior Garang, had had John pulled from the front line, arrested without charge, interrogated and tortured.

Eventually John was released, but at that point he knew that if he stayed in South Sudan he would most likely not survive the war. Not only had he pushed the limits of luck in front-line engagements, but now he was also threatened by his own side.

The day after our reunion, John explained to me how the Dinka-Bor had been treated by the SPLA, and that he was taking Elizabeth's family so he could resettle them somewhere safe in Africa. He also said that, with the help of his Christian god, he and Elizabeth would eventually try to get to a western country and live western lives, where they could live freely, prosperously and happily.

I didn't really understand what living a western life was, and I really didn't understand what it was to prosper and live freely, but when John said that he wanted to take me with him, I was excited by his enthusiasm.

'You are young enough that you don't have to have a life that is only war. You could have a career if you wanted to, Deng. You're smart, and you work hard. You could still have an education.'

Since the moment back in our village when Adut had lied to me and told me I was going to get an education in Ethiopia, I had often thought about what an education might be. My real dream was of going back to the front line, though. I had no desire to leave the war, but I didn't want to leave John either. Finding a brother again reminded me of how strong family bonds could be, and John, in particular, was such a dynamic influence.

He said the first stop in our journey would be the giant refugee camp Kakuma, in northern Kenya. I had actually thought of trying to make it to Kakuma before. A lot of boys from Nattinger had tried to escape to Kakuma, but from what I could tell, success rates had been low. Some had been killed on the way, but more had been returned by the SPLA after having been severely beaten.

It was because of John's persuasiveness that I agreed to go with him. With his stripes on his shoulder and confidence in his step, he walked into my barracks and ordered the commanding officer to allow me to travel to Lokichogio for further treatment for my wounds.

The officers at Nattinger would have no part of it. I'd been on unrestricted duties for months, and they'd seen me playing football most days. The request was not only refused, it most likely created a healthy amount of suspicion. John decided we would be leaving the next night. To stay longer would be dangerous for us both.

When the time came, I felt little of the drama of the moment. For me, it was just another moment of randomness in the story of my childhood. If we succeeded, I would just be in another camp, hungry and sick, yearning to be fighting. If we didn't make it, I would be beaten and sent back to the menial duties of Nattinger life, yearning to be fighting.

For John, though, this moment could mean a life free of war and poverty, not just for him but for his wife. It could also mean death.

On the day of our escape, I considered backing out. Leaving in this way felt like I was avoiding the battlefield that I craved so badly. A hatred of cowardice had been drummed into my every cell, and escaping seemed like a coward's act.

I wondered if I could ask the officers if I would ever be allowed to fight again, and if the answer was no then I would leave. But I realised I couldn't do that. That would show my brother's hand. John was my older brother, and seniority had meant a lot to the boy who had once lived on the White Nile.

That night I was scheduled to be on sentry duty from 8 p.m. to 4 a.m. We planned to flee the base at 3 a.m. I manned my station until my shift was close to being done before I quietly slipped back to the barracks. I tucked my AK-47 into my bed, bunched my blankets so it might look to an uninterested eye like I was still sleeping, and then I fled to Elizabeth's mother's house.

There I met John and the others, and we piled into a truck that John had arranged for us. At that point in the war, both strategic allies and humanitarian benefactors were supplying much of the food that was being consumed by the SPLA, and many of the officers were taking the opportunity to sell that food in Kenya or Uganda to either buy more munitions or line their pockets.

The truck John had arranged was full of sacks of corn; sacks that were supposed to end up in South Sudanese mouths but were destined for sale in Kenya.

As we left Nattinger, John and the members of Elizabeth's family – all holders of papers that allowed them to move freely towards Kenya – rode in the cabin of the truck. I, who was paperless, hid behind the sacks of corn.

It was a twelve-hour journey from Nattinger to Kakuma, and I spent all of it either bouncing around or stationary at checkpoints, of which there were many. At each checkpoint the guards seemed uninterested in the truck and its contents – there was just some perfunctory conversation and then we were off again.

When we arrived in Lokichogio, we said goodbye to Elizabeth's family and wished them well, and then we started walking as briskly as we could manage south, away from the influence of the SPLA and towards the mass of humanity that was Kakuma refugee camp.

Twenty-one

LIFE AT A REFUGEE CAMP

Kakuma refugee camp had been set up in 1991, primarily to support the flood of people fleeing the war in Sudan. But by the time John and I got there it was accommodating people fleeing at least six other wars. Virtually possessionless and penniless, the two of us walked to the intake area of the camp and, eventually, were registered as official refugees.

Here my official refugee life started, which was almost indiscernible from a great part of the life I'd lived as a soldier. There was more food in Kenya, but not much. There was some medicine, and it was greatly needed. There were no bombings, but there was very little hope.

We were taken to an area of Dinka-Bor refugees, and there we found Elizabeth, as well as people who had been there since the very beginning of the war. There was talk of some people being resettled in places like Canada and America, and even Australia, but it wasn't happening to the people around us. It only took a few weeks for all of us to yearn for a life other than the one we were living in Kakuma.

In the many dusty days at Kakuma, I dreamed of being back in a fighting brigade, facing the guns of the Arabs. Without my AK-47 I felt naked.

I asked John if he wanted to go back to the war. He said he didn't. He said we'd taken our first step towards a new life and all he was thinking about was the steps that would follow. He wasn't just looking out for me; he and Elizabeth were now expecting a child.

I believed what he said, as every day he hustled and worked to get us out of Kakuma. Every day my brother was meeting people to find out how an application for external residency could become a reality. John used all the English he had learnt when he was a Bible student to find out everything he could about making an application for an international visa. There was no man or woman, black or white, he would not press to find out how we could get out of the camp. John also travelled out of the camp, often as far as the Kenyan capital, Nairobi, more than 700 kilometres south, where he would petition and apply and harangue to try to increase the likelihood of us being relocated.

John was away in Nairobi when his first son was born, and the boy was delivered into Elizabeth's arms, and mine. Elizabeth named the boy Joshua but, as tribal law dictated, the name would not be permanent until John returned. When he did come back, John had no objection to his wife's choice.

Shortly after meeting his son, John was back in Nairobi. While John hustled outside of the camp, I hustled inside, hunting around the camp for discarded tin cans and turning them into small stoves, which I sold so that Elizabeth, Joshua and I could augment our daily rations.

John came back from the capital unsuccessful in his mission but with strengthened resolve. He'd heard that our chances of relocation might be improved by moving to one of the two enormous refugee camps, Dadaab and Ifo, closer to the Somali border.

It was a long and hungry journey to those two camps and, in both, we found more than 100,000 Somalis fleeing another civil war, which had started in the 1980s and was yet to end.

There were Sudanese at both camps, but our numbers were small and the militant Somali groups in the camp, who had no problems bringing their weapons into the supposedly demilitarised camps, hated us.

There was gunfire most nights in those camps. When I heard the snap of the bullets it would anger me greatly; what a pointless waste it would be to die in a war that wasn't even mine! The gunfire usually came from a group called Al-Shifta, which would later become internationally famous as the militant group Al-Shabaab.

Al-Shifta would sometimes sweep through the Sudanese part of those camps, firing in the air and asserting their dominance. All the Sudanese could do was to flee.

One night in the Ifo camp, when the guns started to rattle and my countrymen and women started to run, I decided that if the Al-Shifta wished to kill me then I would let them. I would not be running any more.

I lay in my cot as the Islamists swept through the camp, and I waited for a bullet. No Al-Shifta men came into my tent that night, though. They just rolled past me, like an unbroken wave.

When the Al-Shifta men disappeared, John returned and berated me. He told me I had lost my memory of what a life was worth, and I told him he had lost his memory of what pride was. He told me I was an idiot and I told him he was a coward.

At that word, 'coward', John went into a rage and beat me very badly. It was the first and last time he ever beat me, and it was brutal.

It's common for Sudanese parents and older siblings to beat young children when they step out of line, but I wouldn't accept a beating from John. I was a soldier, not some child. Yes, he was my older brother, but I was not well practised at being a younger brother, or a family member at all. It had been so long since I had felt a part of a family. The beating didn't just anger me, it confused me and I simply couldn't accept it.

After the beating, John left me, upset. I washed the blood away from my face, went to one of the holes in the camp fence and walked out into the dark. I was hundreds and hundreds of kilometres from the South Sudanese border, but my vague goal was to make it there. Perhaps I would stop when I got to Kakuma, but I didn't know. I just wanted to be away from John.

After four or five hours walking I was spotted by relatives and taken back to the camp. When John and I were reunited there was no real reconciliation. I long harboured real hatred for him after he beat me, but an acceptance came, born of necessity. We were stuck together, for the time being.

Twenty-two

LEARNING ENGLISH

Eventually John decided that we were unlikely to be found to be international refugees in the eastern camps, so he announced we would return to Kakuma. The journey took us several weeks.

I don't know how, but John still managed to maintain hope, and every day he forced me to learn new English words and phrases, which he insisted I would need in my new country.

'Good morning.'

'Thank you very much.'

'Nice to meet you.'

'It is a lovely day.'

I took it all onboard while life at Kakuma continued. John, for his part, never ceased in his efforts to find a way out. There was no person John wouldn't ask about processing or sponsoring, no lead he wouldn't chase to the very end, no matter how weak it was.

John met a *kawaja* woman, a counsellor from Australia who was trying to help people in the camp with their bad dreams and sad faces. The woman, who said she wasn't helping as much as she had hoped, was a Christian, like John, and they would have long conversations about God, the war and Australia.

John became very excited when he heard that this woman, whose name was Christine Harrison, had decided to help one of the people in the camp leave the camp life we were half-living and resettle them in Australia. 'I can't spend all of this time here and not help at least one of you,' she had said to John.

John had heard that Christine was married, so he assumed he would have to get the approval of Christine's husband before she could do anything. He asked Christine for her husband's phone number.

With that number in hand, John set off to the only place where he knew he could make a phone call, Nairobi, 700 kilometres away.

John must have believed strongly in this lead because, before he left, he made me promise that I would sneak into the organised English classes for refugees who were on the verge of emigration.

John had taught me those few English phrases and I already had a jumble of languages in my head – Arabic, Amharic, Dinka, Nuer – but I often didn't know the source of the words I was using. When I started those classes, I was happy to find that a lot of the words I had been using in my country were actually from the English language.

I enjoyed learning what English words I could, but only for the joy of learning, not because I thought much about their application, like John did.

I had little understanding of the life that the people who were moving on after their English lessons were to be living. John talked about America and Australia, but those places meant little to me, except that I had enjoyed the *digigstralia* so much.

I was still, in my mind, a soldier. My mind could not escape the war.

It took some weeks for John to return from making that phone call in Nairobi, and when he came back he had fresh injuries, including a broken skull. He had had the extreme misfortune to be in the Kenyan capital at the same time as some of his factional rivals from the SPLA, including Dr John Garang's son, Mabior.

John was grabbed off the street, blindfolded and taken to a house in the outer suburbs of Nairobi.

There, Mabior and his friends tortured him, leaving him for dead. But he wasn't, and when he regained consciousness, John dragged himself to a clinic and was treated. When he returned to us in Kakuma, many days later, he was a broken and battered man.

Though physically broken, John was upbeat. He had spoken to Christine's husband, Bob, and even though Bob had not heard of his wife's plans to help a refugee, he said he would get the wheels in motion for us to gain Australian visas.

Despite John's words of hope, I saw his new wounds and I became even more convinced that the war would never end for us. I felt hatred for the men who had tortured and conspired to kill my brother.

The Australians, Bob and Christine, were true to their word. For us to be relocated, they would need to guarantee John accommodation, a job and the price of a flight to Sydney for him and his dependants. With the help of their church, they managed to fulfil all of those requirements. A little less than six months after John had returned from Nairobi, we were told to head south to the capital, where we would be given Australian visas.

I tried to share John and Elizabeth's excitement. I tried, but I couldn't. Perhaps it was a fear of change that I had developed the day I was taken from my mother. Perhaps it was because there was too much war still in my blood. I don't know what it was, but I felt nothing while John and Elizabeth were vibrating with happiness.

We were relocated temporarily to Nairobi, and I had never seen such a place, with more cars on the road than I had ever seen cows in a field. There was so much food, too – all types of meat and fruit and vegetables and milk. It seemed that there was no need to be hungry in Nairobi.

The day before we left for Australia, a cousin of ours, who had ascended through the SPLA ranks, visited us. His name was Makuei Deng and he was a general, but even that elevated rank had not kept him safe from the internal friction that perpetually plagued the SPLA. General Makuei had also suffered torture at the hands of the SPLA. He was in Nairobi receiving treatment for various wounds.

When John explained to the general where we would be resettling, Makuei told me I must be prepared for cold like I had never experienced before. I, like most of my people, hate the cold, and seeing the trepidation on my face, the general produced a gift.

'The cold is only to be feared when equipped with the wrong clothes. Take this,' he said, handing over a woollen vest.

On that day I was fourteen years of age, and, quite often, I still like to add a vest to my suit!

Twenty-three

WELCOME TO AUSTRALIA

Even though the war in Sudan had been raging for years, we were only the third Sudanese family to enter Australia as refugees.

We flew to Sydney with Cathay Pacific, and I hated every moment of it. From Nairobi to Hong Kong the drone of the engine noise drove me mad, and we were hungry throughout the flight, as we never figured out how to eat the plastic-covered food that was brought to us, and we were too timid to ask any questions of the flight attendants.

When we got to Hong Kong we were delivered to a transit lounge, and there we sat in silence while Asian people stared at us and whispered. We were too scared to even speak to each other. I'd never met an Asian person before, and knew nothing about them.

What did they want from us? Should I be scared of them? It was all too confusing to fathom.

The flight to Sydney was similarly difficult, and once again we were not able to figure out how to eat the food on that leg. Then we landed in Australia – a place that was as strange to me as Neptune may be to you. There were giant illuminated signs, and everything was clean. A lot of people were frowning, and everybody looked exactly the same – except for one very large, round man with a grey beard who was waiting for us when we emerged from customs.

This was Bob, the man who John had travelled more than 700 kilometres to speak to on the phone, and who, with his wife, had changed the trajectories of our lives. Bob had a smile that poured out of his beard, and woollen jumpers for all of us in his hands.

As we walked out of the airport doors, I was hit with a cold I had never before felt. I rushed to get my jumper over my body, tucking my hands up against my stomach. John asked Bob where we were going now, and Bob told him we were going to a place called Blacktown. John's face sank as though he had just spied an SPLA roadblock. He assumed Blacktown was the Kakuma of Sydney – a dusty ghetto where all of the arriving black people would be dumped.

John eventually asked Bob how long we would have to stay in Blacktown, and Bob said we'd be there for a few days, to set ourselves up, and then we could visit him in the Blue Mountains. That sounded much nicer.

Bob said he liked Blacktown and that we'd probably like it there.

After leaving the airport he drove us straight to a restaurant called McDonald's, which was a palace of confusion for me. There were tables of wood that weren't made of wood, and people dressed up in uniforms who weren't soldiers, and there were huge pictures of food pasted on the walls . . . only I couldn't see where the food actually was.

John said that Bob would arrange for the food to be brought to us. Bob spoke to one of the people in uniform and, after a short while, food was brought out on trays.

I had a hamburger – I don't remember which one – and it was perhaps the strangest thing I had ever eaten. I was hungry, though, so I wolfed it down along with the yellow potato strings that accompanied it. When we finished our meal, Bob drove us to this Blacktown, which was absolutely nothing like Kakuma.

Bob worked for a charity called Marist Youth Care, and he had arranged an apartment for us above their offices, which had previously been a convent adjacent to a school and church. It was a small, two-bedroom place, but for us it was a palace, filled with technological wonders and food the likes of which we hadn't even known existed.

After the long journey to Australia, I laid my body down on the first real bed I'd ever seen, under my first duvet, and I slept in a country at peace.

I will, for the rest of my life, be grateful to the people and organisations of Western Sydney for welcoming me into their fold. I especially appreciate everything the Marists did for us – from flying us over to arranging a job for John as the caretaker of the grounds surrounding our apartment.

Things were not easy in those early days, though. Everything from crossing the road to heating the oven (Elizabeth tried to heat it with kindling and fire) was confusing to us. After a couple of days in Blacktown, Bob was true to his word and took us to his and Christine's house in the Blue Mountains, where we met their family.

Bob and Christine took us for a walk into the bush, and my heart filled when I saw rock formations that looked like home. Even though the rocks and mountains looked more like Eastern Equatoria, I started to think about the Nile, and my village.

I thought about my mother. It had been almost a decade since I'd seen her, and I wondered what she looked like, if she was even alive. Even now it's almost impossible to get information from the villages, let alone then, while the war was still raging. I had trouble remembering her face, or a situation I could place her in. It no longer felt like a real place, my village, nor did this new place with its yellow string potatoes and the white people who all looked like one another. Even the war had started to stop feeling real, and that made me sad.

Although I had a general sense of unease, a good part of that day in the bush was actually quite nice. John, Elizabeth and their son Joshua were happy, and the sun was shining, which felt good on my skin, and Bob was so kind and friendly. When the sun went down, though, and the winter air started to chill, the little happiness I'd felt left me.

There is no summer or winter in the south of Sudan, there is only the hot wet and the hot dry. The first real winter night I'd ever experienced was in the Blue Mountains, and it was a freezing one.

I was unaccustomed to being inside a building, but in the Blue Mountains I couldn't go outside either, because when I did my skin would feel like it was starting to burn. I had never in my life been cold before, let alone that cold.

When I woke and rose, it was possibly even colder than when I'd gone to bed. There was frost underfoot and, as I walked around Bob's yard, it crunched. I had never seen ice before. The cold was my enemy. I disliked the way it stopped my mouth from working and turned my breath into smoke; it was all so unnatural.

That morning, if I could have clicked my fingers and been transported back to Kakuma, or even Nattinger, I would have done it without a thought.

The next day, John and I tried to register with Centrelink – the Australian social security service – and we found that they were not well set up for African refugees.

As a minor, I would need a legal guardian in Australia, which was a strange concept for me because the closest I'd had to a guardian since the age of seven were superior officers from the SPLA. For my brother to be my guardian, he and I had to have the same surname, or at least a good reason why we didn't. Dinka-Bor naming convention was apparently not a good reason.

John's full name was John Mac Acuek, so for us to register with the refugee papers that we had been given in Kenya, I had to adopt John's surname.

When I was given my Centrelink accreditation, I found a name on the form that meant absolutely nothing to me and bore no similarity to the names my family gave me, nor any mention of my clan's history.

'This is not my name. This is nobody's name and it means nothing,' I told John, holding up my Centrelink ID bearing the name 'Dave Machacuek'.

'If Dave Machacuek gets to eat food and go to school, then I would want to be him,' replied John.

Twenty-four

MY WESTERN EDUCATION BEGINS

A few days after I received my Centrelink ID, 'Dave Machacuek' was enrolled to be a student at Evans High School in Blacktown. I turned up that freezing morning at the high school confused, and suffered silently through Literature, Mathematics and Human Biology classes.

I spoke to no students, understood nothing that the teachers said, and yearned for the day to end. I was fifteen years old then, and that was the first day of traditional schooling I had ever undertaken. It was not what I'd expected.

When I got home I told John I could not do another day like that. I told my brother I would not sit in those classes while the white people stared and the teachers droned on in what to me sounded like gibberish. I told John I was still angry at being called Dave, too, and would no longer answer to that name.

John knew I was adamant – this was not just teenage discontent. John could be a hard man, but he did not lack compassion either. He told me he would make sure that I could change my name back, and he realised that they were not going to teach me what I really needed to learn at Evans High School. First I needed to learn English.

For the time being I stayed at home. I didn't want to go outside at all, really, for I would get looks everywhere I went, and I didn't even know how to cross the road. So I spent most of the first couple of weeks in Australia sitting on the floor with Joshua, watching a television show (a rare luxury in Kakuma) called *The Wiggles*.

It turned out I didn't have to leave the house to get myself into trouble, however. When we first got to the apartment, one of the Marists explained how everything worked. When they got to the microwave they explained it to John and me as 'a box that heats up food'. Like a fire, right? I understood that.

The Marists delivered some groceries for us, including cans of Coca-Cola which they put in the fridge. I decided that I'd have one of the cans. Having never had a cold drink before, I decided to warm it up in the box that heats up food.

The can exploded in the microwave, but not before creating a terrifying, localised electrical storm that I thought would destroy the apartment. I was scared of the microwave after that, and felt like an idiot, until Elizabeth did the exact same thing a couple of weeks later!

After a few weeks of staying in the apartment and playing with Josh, John arranged for me to start an intensive English course at Blacktown TAFE.

That first day at TAFE was really my first day as a student. When I sat down in class I was confused: all of the people in my class were white, and I had assumed that all white people were able to speak English. It turned out that not all white people could speak English, and also that a lot of the people in that class were not white at all but were Indian or South East Asian. They had all looked like *kawaja* to me.

Most of the people studying the course were as lacking in English language skills as I was, so I had finally found a place in Australia that didn't confuse me. A place where I fitted in. We were all learning together.

As I managed to get a handle on my first English letters, and my mouth around some single-syllabled words, I started to feel a sense of achievement. It felt good.

I would study every night with John, showing him my workbooks and getting help from him on my answers, and place the words I had learnt into a context I understood. I pretended my TAFE work was a chore, but the truth was it was the one thing I was enjoying in Australia.

Unfortunately, the war was still deep inside of me. I barely slept when I got to Australia, because when I did sleep I would have vivid and dynamic Sudanese nightmares. Sometimes I would be back assaulting Kapoeta, or running from the bombs, but often the nightmares would be less literal, with me being pursued by something that I couldn't quite discern, or manically running to find something that I'd lost. The two themes in my nightmares were running, and a fear of something worse than death. Often I would wake up somewhere other than my bed, having run into a wall or some furniture.

My insomnia would spur me to ask for more and more TAFE work. During the day it was easy to fill my head with television and school, and play with my nephew, but at night, in the dark, my head would only go to the bad places – places that were only slightly better than the places I went to when I was asleep.

On Sundays, John would make me go to church with Bob and Elizabeth, but I wasn't one for sitting down for long periods of time while being lectured in a language I could barely understand. The people there were very nice and welcoming, though, and I made my first Australian friend there: Geoff Hicherson, a large, retired police detective who used to work out of Blacktown Local Area Command. The first time I went to church, Geoff bounded up to us, introduced himself and his family – Geoff had two sons, Paul and Ian, who were roughly the same age as me, and a wife, Margaret, just as kind as he – and started talking to me. Even though I couldn't understand a word he was saying, the smiles and greetings spoke a universal language of kindness. I loved being in Geoff's company.

Partly through mime and partly through broken English, Geoff asked me what kind of things I liked to do, and I told him that I liked to play soccer. Geoff immediately arranged for me to start football training with his son Paul. He would pick me up from the apartment before training and drop me home at the end of it. And, more often than not, he would arrange a meal for me. He did it all from the kindness of his heart. The war I'd left seemed like such a large thing, and the charity of a churchman and his football-playing son a small thing by comparison, but Geoff's kindness was so valuable to me.

While I understood almost no aspects of Australian life, I understood soccer – the goals and the ball, the offside rule and the joy of scoring, in the exact same way every Australian player did.

Paul was an excellent soccer player. When I started training with him I demonstrated some raw usefulness but little polish. I was very fast, though, and fit, and soon I was training with Paul's excellent club side, the Fairfield Bulls.

Our coach was a man named Marshall Soper, a former Socceroos player, whose strict discipline and impressive expertise reminded me of Commander Majok. Training under Marshall was exactly what I needed in my life. He was an Australian man whom I respected and didn't want to disappoint. That football training was a good connection between the discipline of military life and Australian life, and each session put a little bit more purpose into my life.

After I started playing football, my TAFE English studies went from strength to strength. I'd do all of my homework quickly and then lie on the lounge room floor with little Joshua watching *The Wiggles*. These Wiggles were of particular use for me in learning English. The slow way they spoke, and the comic exaggeration they used, helped me understand all the words they were using. Sometimes I found myself watching Josh's Wiggles DVDs without him!

At football training, players would sometimes catch me singing 'Big Red Car' or 'Hot Potato, Hot Potato' to myself, and laugh. I didn't care. Apart from football, the only thing I really cared about then was learning English.

Twenty-five

FINDING FRIENDS

I didn't yet value how good life was in Australia – too much of the war was still in me. I found it hard to give thanks to John for taking me away from East Africa.

If I'd recognised that, perhaps I might have recognised how difficult John was finding life in Australia. John and I bickered sometimes, we argued other times and, on rare occasions, we fought bitterly.

On those occasions, Geoff and Margaret welcomed me into their house, giving me a meal and a bed for the night. Geoff was an excellent, patient teacher and from him I learnt a lot about language and the Australian way of life.

When I was at home, I would consume the English language like fire does a dry tree. I'd sometimes do my TAFE homework two or three times, and after that I would read passages from the Bible and then recite them in long, fast, rote strings, like a chant. I would stay awake as long as I could, mumbling those passages to myself, trying to stave off the nightmares.

I thought the nightmares would become more infrequent the longer I was in Australia, but that wasn't the case. Soon I managed to make my days so full I barely thought about Sudan, but at night I couldn't help but think about bombs and guns and dead bodies. Especially when I fell asleep.

The church people suggested I try counselling, and I did try one session but very quickly surmised that they couldn't do anything for me. I wasn't really ready to speak, and the counsellor I spoke to was not equipped to help me with the kinds of things that I had done and seen. I knew it would be strong men like Geoff, Bob and Marshall who would help me assimilate into modern life and help me put my demons behind me.

I remember an instance at one of those early church visits when Geoff gave me a twenty-dollar note. I asked what it was for and he explained that the money was to go into my back pocket, not for fun or food, but for an occasion when it was actually needed. He said I would know that moment when it arrived.

That occasion would come just a couple of weeks later when I was attempting to catch a train for the first time. I had never seen a train before, let alone caught one, so I walked into Blacktown station as confused as a puppy in a thunderstorm. I didn't really understand about timetables and tickets and routes.

After some time I figured out which train I wanted to take, and when it was arriving. When the doors opened, I jumped onboard without having solved the ticket conundrum. A few stations later, some ticket inspectors stopped me.

When they started asking questions I couldn't understand, I began to think that perhaps they would take me to jail or maybe even send me back to Sudan. Eventually I got them to call Geoff, and he explained my situation. When we got off, they showed me how to buy a ticket, which I did with the twenty dollars Geoff had given me. Since then I have always paid for whatever I am supposed to pay for.

That moment felt like a cultural breakthrough. I wasn't admonished or beaten by the ticket inspectors who found me, I was helped, and I was proud when I managed to purchase my first train ticket.

The problem was, however, that for every problem I solved, another turned up. Even as my English improved quickly, everything about Australian life was still so confusing, from buying food in a supermarket to crossing a busy intersection.

For the first few months in Australia I lived a very limited life. The paths I took to TAFE or my apartment, or to Geoff's, or to the fields where I played football, were always the same because, on the routes I took, people expected me.

Blacktown is now quite flush with Sudanese people, but back then, seeing a boy with such dark skin was a novelty. I hadn't ever stood out in South Sudan, and I didn't like the surprise I saw in people's faces when they noticed me in Sydney.

When I walked on the footpath, it felt like everyone stared and pointed and whispered. It was especially hard for me when I had to go into businesses owned by Arabic people, who I'd been taught my whole life were killers and the enemy. I'd feel their eyes burning into me with their stares.

As far as I knew, there were only two other African families in Sydney then, a North Sudanese family who we had little in common with, and a Dinka family from the state of Bahr el Ghazal who used to visit our apartment from time to time. Due to the rules of seniority, and because they had no children my age, it was really only John who spent time talking with that family.

Then, one day, I saw an African guy walking down the street in Blacktown. I cut across the road and intercepted him.

'Deng Adut,' I said, putting my hand out.

'Lamin Colley,' he replied, not at all taken aback by my forwardness.

That was it – we were mates, and I have been close to Lamin ever since.

Lamin worked at Woolworths full time and had his own apartment, so soon I was spending more time with him than with John, Elizabeth and Josh. Lamin and I usually watched the English Premier League, and he helped me with my English homework.

My English was too limited for us to actually hold a conversation, but we appreciated each other's company enough that it didn't matter. We often used to speak to each other in gibberish – a mishmash of real words in many languages, and made-up sounds – just to feel as though we were speaking like friends would. I used to devour those conversations of nonsense. I'd forgotten what it was like to have a contemporary.

Over the next few weeks and months, Lamin and I started to find – usually at soccer matches – more and more African teenagers to make friends with. There was Mickeyas, an Ethiopian; Aji, a Ghanian; Joseph and Robert Awalla, two South Sudanese brothers; and another South Sudanese teen named Richard Aconda, who'd been in Australia since the 1980s. We are all still friends today.

Lamin's apartment ended up serving as an informal drop-in centre for the African youth of Blacktown, and I spent hour upon hour there, enjoying the company of people who understood me.

Richard especially was a huge help for me. Not only was his English first class, he also spoke Juba Arabic, a language I'd picked up a lot of during the war. My English improved in leaps and bounds at that time, and having a place where I felt accepted also helped me emotionally.

There was only one place we spent more time at than Lamin's apartment, and that was the soccer field at Blacktown Workers Club. If I wasn't sleeping or eating or studying, I was playing football at that field.

At first we played every day until sunset, but after we found the switch that turned on the flood-lights we played deep into the night. When we could literally play no more we would head back to Lamin's apartment for a barbecue feast and long, involved discussions about the intricacies of the English language. Those African boys became the bedrock of my Australian life.

Learning English wasn't an impossible task, just a very difficult one, and thankfully I had the help that I needed. I had my African friends, I had Josh and the Wiggles, and I had Geoff, who would drive all of us African misfits to our football games while grilling us about verbs, nouns and adjectives.

If I had had an Australian godfather, it would have been Geoff.

Twenty-six

MY FIRST JOB

My brother John took all the measures he could to make life better for his family in those early years in Australia. He undertook his own TAFE course – one that would not only teach him English but potentially give him a tertiary entrance qualification – while also diligently fulfilling his caretaker position. But even when he was a student and a worker, he never really managed to feel comfortable in Australia.

When he finished his TAFE course John quickly directed his attention to a university degree. He was accepted to study Social Science at Western Sydney University. We were delighted for him, but not surprised; when John saw a path, he would move heaven and earth to make sure he could walk it.

The path John saw for himself involved working on large international aid projects. He saw a middle-class dream in his future, but he would also never forget the African nightmare of his past. He couldn't forget how easily and cheaply lives could be improved in Sudan, and he wanted to be in a position to do just that . . . only not in Sudan – never in Sudan, and preferably not in Africa. John had always thought Africa would kill him if he returned. He had his sights set on East Timor instead.

That didn't mean he didn't care about the plight of his tribe and the people he loved. When news about the war in Sudan was available (often it wasn't, as it was a war that the west largely ignored), he and his friends – the Sudanese refugee population in Australia was starting to grow – would endlessly consume information about the fighting and potential treaties.

For my part, those stories of treaties and alliances and international pressure meant almost nothing. I had never seen the war from the perspective of the eagle, I had only ever seen it through the eyes of the warthog – on the ground in the day-to-day grind of being a soldier.

In 2001 there was another sharp improvement in my English abilities, and that was the year I became confident conversing with strangers in English.

I started to feel like I'd managed to tap into regular Australian life.

The charms of a western life were starting to reveal themselves. My mind would still go back to Africa in my nightmares, but when I was awake I was concerned only with the English Premier League standings, or when my mates were going to be heading to Lamin's place, or what English homework I still had to do.

Around that time I got my first job, which was arranged by Geoff. It was a lawn-mowing gig at a large house in Minchinbury, and my efforts paid me twenty dollars at first, then twenty-five, and finally thirty, in recognition of the extreme care I took in the presentation of that garden.

Later that year I did some modelling, too, which helped me put a lot more than twenty dollars in my pocket. Then, again with the help of Geoff, I got a job at a petrol station in Blacktown. As he drove me to the interview, Geoff explained to me that this would be the perfect job for me. Not only would it help with my conversational English, I could do all my shifts at night, if I so chose. Geoff bought me a second-hand bike so I could get to and from the petrol station.

The job did improve my English as I worked more and more shifts, but it also gave me more of an understanding of the complexity of Australian society. For the most part, people were respectful and friendly, but there were some people who were as furious and aggressive as some of the angrier soldiers I had met in Sudan.

I was robbed one night at work. A gun was thrust in my face – not something I'd ever expected to have happen to me in Australia. It was quite late – maybe 2 or 3 a.m. – and a drug addict wearing a hoodie burst into the station with a handgun and threatened me. He wanted the money from the till in front of me, which I gave to him. Then he wanted more money. He grabbed my tie, pointed the gun at my belly and screamed for me to get him the money from the second till.

That second till was heavy with coins, and when the man motioned for me to dump the coins into a cradle he'd made with both his hands in his hoodie, I decided I would give him the money then grab the gun.

Then I looked hard at the handgun and saw that it wasn't even loaded. This man was committing a robbery with an unloaded gun! I had no interest in a fistfight with a drug addict, so I gave the man his meagre spoils and let him leave. I didn't understand why anyone would find themselves in so desperate a spot when living in a place like Australia. It made no sense to me.

It was during the period that I was working at the petrol station that I also first experienced the sharp sting of racism. As many of the other African boys also worked at night and on weekends, our days off would often end up being during the week, and in spring and summer we'd pile into a car or two and make the trek to Bondi Beach.

One day we parked a few streets away from the beach, and as we walked to the sand an older, white Australian man took it upon himself to start yelling abuse at us. We ignored him and avoided a confrontation, but I began to think about the abuse he had hurled at my friends and me. I realised that no matter how much work I did to become an Australian, there would be some people who would never accept me. Even if I assimilated in every way, the darkness of my skin would preclude me from being considered Australian by a select group of Australians.

In 2001 I finished my TAFE course and received a qualification that was the equivalent of the Higher School Certificate. I could now start to think about further education, and possibly even a vocation.

I'd only ever thought about doing three things with my life – fighting, fishing and raising cattle – but I knew I didn't want a career in Australia doing any of those things. The problem was, I didn't have any idea of what else I could do.

Then, one day, an Italian friend from my football club told me that his son was about to enrol in a one-year accounting course, and that I would do well to do the same. I told him I thought it was unlikely that I'd be able to keep up with a course like that, but this friend promised that he and his son would help make sure that I passed.

John told me I should do the course. 'It's with help that people like us will get ahead,' he told me. 'If help is there from someone you trust, you grab it with both hands.' It was a very Sudanese way of looking at things, as it's through clan or tribal connections that almost everything gets done back in Sudan.

I told John that I thought I didn't have the language skills or scholarly instinct to do accounting, but John disagreed.

So I enrolled in an Advanced Diploma in Accounting the next day. It was an important time for both my brother and me. While I was starting my academic life, John was trying to begin his professional life. Yet, despite being a man of incredible drive and intelligence, who spoke six languages, John could find no work except in a factory in Penrith. With each shift in that job, John's confidence started to erode, ground down by life's unfairness – an unfairness he thought he'd escaped by coming to Australia.

John never stopped trying, though – attending meetings, sending résumés and petitioning aid organisations. The offers eventually came in, but only for work in East Africa, where John decided to return.

For my part, I threw myself into my accounting course and found it difficult. True to his word, though, my Italian friend and his son never let me get too far behind, taking me back to their place many nights after school and filling me with coffee and study until I had caught up. Even though I completed the course with moderate grades, I wasn't sure this was going to be the path for me. The Marist Brothers' charity group gave me a full-time job in their accounting department, and I tried hard at the job because I appreciated the opportunity to help an organisation that had done so much for me, but there were never going to be any songs about my incredible book-balancing. Perhaps it was time for me to think about what I actually wanted for my life.

It seemed that for much of my life up until that point I'd been subject to the volition of others – be they the SPLA, or John. Maybe now it was time to think about what I actually wanted from this new Australian start.

I worked enough to be able to afford my own apartment, and started to think about my family back in Sudan. The political situation had changed. On 9 January 2005, after twenty-two years of constant war, in which an estimated two million people were killed, legal peace had come to Sudan. An agreement was drawn up stipulating that the north could not insist on sharia law in the south – the root cause of the war – and that the north would allow for a referendum on the potential independence of the south. The SPLA, for its part, was to stop attacking the oilfields that would now benefit both north and south, and was to demobilise all of their remaining child soldiers.

When I came to Australia, we were some of only a handful of Sudanese in Sydney, but by the time the peace agreement had been signed six years later, the refugee community had swollen. When the official reconciliation between north and south was announced, the Sudanese diaspora partied through the day and night across Western Sydney, from Sydney Olympic Park to Granville, and of course Blacktown, where the bulk of the Australian–Sudanese had resettled.

We danced, sang Sudanese songs and played football, and I shared food and drink with Nuer and Dinka alike – and even people from the north. It felt like the beginning of a new era.

Twenty-seven

A SON OF SYDNEY

In my lifetime there had never been a time of hope in the south of Sudan like that time. John came back to Sydney after the peace agreement, but by then I realised he was not returning to us in a permanent way.

'There will be a new country, Deng, and that will be my home,' he said.

Before he left I sought John out for advice. I had decided I wanted to apply for a course of university study and I wanted to know which school John thought I should apply for.

John said, 'I'd always seen you as a lawyer.'

'A lawyer?'

'You're a hard worker, Deng. When you set your mind to doing something, you can do it. Including this.'

That was perhaps the last advice I ever took from John, but it was the best.

Sadly he died a few years later in South Sudan, which was a huge blow to me and Elizabeth and John's sons. The country of my birth did not stay peaceful, and the fighting and the killing has continued. I was able to return and see my mother in her village more than once, which brought us both much happiness, and although I wanted her to return with me to the safety of Australia, she did not want to leave the village she'd lived in her whole life.

After many years of hard work, I graduated from law school and became a lawyer. It was then that I felt I was in a position to help refugees who were struggling as I had when I first arrived in Australia. So on top of my work I gave speeches about my experiences. I wanted to honour John's memory and make him proud of all that he had achieved and had helped me achieve. I wanted to explain the circumstances that had brought us to Australia and tell people how hard life had been when we came here. I wanted people to understand that no one ever wants to be a refugee.

In 2016 I was invited to give the Australia Day address. It was a great honour. Although I was daunted by the invitation, I wanted to speak about what Australia meant to me, and what it had meant to John. When I spoke publicly, I very much believed in the usefulness of what I spoke about. I knew that people came to hear about war and sadness and a past that was so unusual for them, but I also knew that they left thinking about how normal my present was – and how much I was like them.

My skin is much darker than most Australians', and my accent is still quite thick, but I am an Australian just like they are. The only real difference is that I had to fight to become Australian. I thought it important to relate that fact to as many people as possible.

If you can relate to me – a reformed child soldier coming from one of the most isolated and disadvantaged nations on earth – then there are few refugees in Australia you can't relate to. And if you relate to them, you can have compassion for them and their circumstances.

Despite all that has happened to me, as I said at the beginning of this book, I know I was born lucky, and I stayed lucky.

I feel as though I have lived three lives. I have lived as a Dinka, ruled by custom and the big god *Nhialic*. I have lived as a soldier ruled by maniacs and death. I have also lived as an Australian, and law, justice and reason rule that life.

That last life is my true life, and the one I choose to continue. I am more an Australian, and more a lawyer, than I am a soldier or Dinka, but I will also forever be South Sudanese. My skin will never change, and I shall never completely lose my accent.

If I ever see the Nile again, and see eagles soaring above it, my heart will skip a beat, no matter how old or grey I may be. My mother will always be my mother, my brother always my brother.

I will leave you with this thought: I believe there are really only two things to do in life – find things you believe in, and then dedicate yourself to them.

I believe in justice and education, but I also believe that all people, including refugees, should be recognised as the people that they are. My hope is that this book will help you to believe the same. Perhaps the songs of my life have a different tone and cadence to yours, but they are about love and hope and yearning and sadness, just like yours.

My hope is that now you know my songs, perhaps one day, when you see my brother, you will also see yours.

If you would like to hear Deng Adut's Australia Day speech titled 'Freedom From Fear', you can find it here:

https://www.australiaday.com.au/events/ australia-day-address/deng-thiak-adut/

Acknowledgements

DENG

Thank you to Elizabeth, George, Joshua and the rest of my family who have accompanied me on this journey. I'm grateful to my dear friends Joe Correy, Caroline Ayling, Lamin Colley and Mickey Negus.

For the guidance I thank Hugh Riminton, Dr Michael Adams, Hon. Terry Buddin SC and Hugh Selby. A big shout out to everyone at Western Sydney University, my colleagues in the legal profession, Vanessa and the team at Hachette, Sally McPherson, my Australian mum Felicity Bennett-Bremner and, of course, to Christine and Bob Harrison. And finally, thank you to my co-writer Ben Mckelvey: it was a wild ride, mate, and I couldn't have done it with anyone but you!

Acknowledgements

BEN

I'd like to thank Elizabeth, Hugh, Vanessa and Peggy for their invaluable help in Australia, and Ajak, Philip, and Mikeyas for their essential support in Africa. Most of all I'd like to thank Deng, who managed to bring light to even the darkest corners of this story.

hachette
CHILDREN'S BOOKS

If you would like to find out more about
Hachette Children's Books, our authors, upcoming events
and new releases you can visit our website,
Facebook or follow us on Twitter:

hachettechildrens.com.au
twitter.com/HCBoz
facebook.com/hcboz

Teachers notes are available from the
Hachette Australia website:
www.hachette.com.au/teachers-and-librarians/